delicious ideas!

# delicious ideas!

The Legacy Cookbook, Second Edition

## Agape International Cathedral
## S.E.E.D. Ministry

J MERRILL

J M E R R I L L

**J Merrill Publishing, Inc.**
434 Hillpine Drive
Columbus, OH 43207
www.JMerrill.pub

**Library of Congress Control Number:** *2024950716*
**Paperback ISBN:** *978-1-961475-33-5*
**Hardcover ISBN:** *978-1-961475-34-2*
**eBook ISBN:** *978-1-961475-35-9*

**Book Title:** *Delicious Ideas!: The Legacy Cookbook*
**Author:** *Agape International Cathedral - Morning Star Missionary Group*
**Cover / Chapter Artwork:** *Your Vision Designed*

### Expression
### Of
### Appreciation

*Our organization wishes to sincerely express our appreciation and thanks to all those individuals who donated recipes, helped with the compiling and the selling or in any other way contributed to the publication of this delightful cookbook.*

**Morning Star Missionary Group**

# table of contents

## Officers in 1982

President ............................................................... Cora Bohanna

Vice President ...................................................... Eva Jordan

Secretary .............................................................. Donna Flournoy

Treasurer ............................................................. Irene Collier

*Morning Star Tabernacle Missionaries*

Members: (Front Row) Irene Collier, Cora Bohanna, Eva Jordan, *Donna Flournoy, *Beverly Rose. (Back Row) Winifred Bondurant, *Ona Goff, Anita Deel, *Kimberly Strain and Rosella Williams

*Committee for Cookbook

# Appetizers, Pickles, Relishes

Delicious Ideas!

## SPICE GUIDE

**Allspice**—Similar to cloves but more pungent and deeply flavored. Enhances the taste of most fruits and adds depth to winter produce like pumpkins and squash.

**Bay Leaf**—Adds a woodsy background note to soups and sauces.

**Caraway Seed**—These anise-flavored seeds are essential for soda bread, sauerkraut, and potato salad.

**Cayenne Pepper**—Made from dried and ground red chili peppers, cayenne pepper adds significant heat to dishes like soups, braises, and spice mixes without altering the core flavors.

**Cinnamon**—A staple in baked goods, cinnamon is also used in savory dishes like Indian curries and Moroccan chicken. It can also be added to hot drinks for extra warmth.

**Cloves**—A sweet and warming spice commonly used in baking but also excellent with braised meats.

**Coriander Seed**—With an earthy, lemony flavor, coriander seed is used in many Mexican and Indian dishes.

**Cumin**—A common ingredient in curries and chili powders, cumin can be used whole or ground right before use. It loses potency quickly but can be revived by toasting in a dry skillet over medium heat.

**Curry Powder**—A blend of cumin, coriander, turmeric, pepper, and chilis.

**Garlic Powder**—Made from dehydrated garlic cloves, garlic powder gives dishes a sweeter, milder garlic flavor.

**Ginger**—Adds unique flavor and texture to stir-fries, roasted meats, and ginger snaps. Fresh ginger should be firm and stays fresh in the refrigerator for up to ten days.

**Mace**—From the same plant as nutmeg, mace is more subtle and delicate, making it excellent in savory dishes, especially stews and homemade sausages.

**Nutmeg**—With a distinctive yet subtle flavor, nutmeg is sweet and pungent and often used in cakes, desserts, custards, and with fruits and vegetables.

**Peppercorn**—Used to season nearly any savory dish, peppercorns come in black, green, or white varieties. Black peppercorns are the most potent. Ground pepper should be used quickly, as it loses flavor within four months.

**Paprika**—Commonly used as a garnish and to add spice, paprika varies in color and flavor from mild to hot and orange to red. Hungarian paprika is considered the highest quality.

**Sage**—With a pine-like flavor and hints of lemon and eucalyptus, sage complements meats, tomato sauces, and bean dishes.

## Sweet and Sour Ham Balls

*Recipe by Ona Goff*

### Ingredients:

1 (16 oz.) can pears, syrup reserved
1 lb. ground ham (leftover)
3/4 cup soft breadcrumbs
1 egg
1 Tbsp grated onion
1/2 tsp prepared horseradish
1/4 tsp dry mustard
1/4 tsp salt

1/8 tsp pepper
1 Tbsp oil
1 Tbsp cornstarch
3 Tbsp brown sugar
1/4 cup vinegar
Dash of salt
1/2 green pepper, cut into strips
1/3 cup water

### Instructions:

1. Drain the pears, reserving the syrup.
2. In a mixing bowl, combine the ham, egg, breadcrumbs, onion, horseradish, mustard, salt, and pepper. Shape into balls.
3. Heat the oil in a skillet and brown the ham balls on all sides.
4. In a separate saucepan, combine the reserved pear syrup, cornstarch, brown sugar, vinegar, water, and a dash of salt. Cook over medium heat, stirring constantly, until the sauce is thick and clear.
5. Add the pear halves, browned ham balls, and green pepper strips to the sauce. Heat for 5 minutes, occasionally basting the pears and ham balls.
6. Serve warm with steamed rice, or offer as hors d'oeuvres with toothpicks.

## Shrimp Cocktail

*Recipe by Gail Morall*

### Ingredients:

2 packages cooked shrimp
Lettuce leaves

Lemon wedges
Cocktail sauce (recipe below)

### Cocktail Sauce:

1/2 cup ketchup
2 Tbsp lemon juice
1 Tbsp grated onion
2 Tbsp mayonnaise

1 tsp Worcestershire sauce
1/4 tsp salt
Dash of pepper

3

Delicious Ideas!

**Instructions:**

1. Arrange lettuce leaves in cocktail glasses. Place shrimp on the lettuce and add cocktail sauce.
2. For the sauce, combine all ingredients and chill before serving.

## Terri's Spinach Omelet Supreme

*Recipe by Terri Bohanna*

**Ingredients:**

| | |
|---|---|
| 1 cup cooked, chopped spinach | 3 eggs |
| 1 cup cooked, chopped ham | Salt, to taste |
| 1/2 cup Swiss cheese, shredded, plus extra for garnish | Pepper, to taste |

**Instructions:**

1. Beat the eggs with a sprinkle of salt and a dash of pepper.
2. Pour the egg mixture into a hot skillet, then add the spinach, ham, and cheese.
3. Roll the mixture into an omelet shape and cook until lightly browned.
4. Remove from skillet and garnish with additional cheese before serving.

## Deviled Beef Wedges

*Recipe by Irene Collier*

**Ingredients:**

| | |
|---|---|
| 9 small muffins | 1 (4 oz.) can deviled ham |
| 1/4 cup butter | 1/4 lb. blue cheese, crumbled |
| 1 lb. ground beef | |

**Instructions:**

1. Split muffins, toast lightly, and spread with butter while hot.
2. Combine the ground beef and deviled ham, then spread the mixture on each muffin half.
3. Sprinkle blue cheese over the meat mixture.
4. Broil for 5–8 minutes, or until cheese is bubbly and meat is cooked to your preference.
5. Cut each muffin into quarters. Yield: 36 wedges.

## Pickled Beets

*Recipe by Eva Jordan*

**Ingredients:**

2 (16 oz.) cans sliced beets, drained (reserve liquid)
1 1/2 cups sugar

3/4 cup vinegar
2 (3-inch) cinnamon sticks

**Instructions:**

1. In a small saucepan, combine the reserved beet liquid, sugar, vinegar, and cinnamon sticks.
2. Bring to a boil, stirring constantly, for about 3 minutes.
3. Pour the hot mixture over the beets and allow to cool.
4. Cover and refrigerate for at least 8 hours.
5. To serve, remove beets with a slotted spoon. Yield: about 3 cups.

## Freezer Pickles

*Recipe by Sharon Wolford*

**Ingredients:**

7 cups cucumber slices
3 medium onions, thinly sliced
1 green pepper, sliced
2 cups sugar

1 cup vinegar
1 Tbsp salt
1 tsp celery seeds

**Instructions:**

1. In a large container, layer the cucumber, onion, and green pepper slices.
2. In a separate bowl, mix the sugar, vinegar, salt, and celery seeds; pour over the vegetables. (Do not add more liquid; it will not cover the pickles completely.)
3. Let stand in the refrigerator for 24 hours.
4. Transfer into plastic containers of your preferred size. Store in the freezer.

## Sweet Pickle Chips

*Recipe by Eva Jordan*

**Ingredients:**

1-gallon sliced cucumber
1 cup pickling salt

3 Tbsp alum
3 tsp ginger

Delicious Ideas!

**Syrup:**

3 lbs. sugar (2 1/2 cups per lb.)
1 quart vinegar
2 Tbsp celery seed

1 cinnamon stick, broken
Pinch of whole cloves

**Instructions:**

1. Place cucumber slices in a large crock. Add salt and cover with boiling water. Let sit for 3 days, then drain.
2. Add alum and enough water to cover. Bring to a boil, then drain.
3. Add water and ginger; bring to a boil again and drain.
4. Prepare the syrup by cooking the syrup ingredients until the sugar is dissolved.
5. Add the cucumber slices to the syrup and cook for 30 minutes.
6. Pour into sterilized jars and seal. Yield: approximately 6 pints.

## Chip and Vegetable Dip

*Recipe by Paul Holliman*

**Ingredients:**

1 cup (8 oz.) sour cream
1 cup Hellmann's mayonnaise
1 Tbsp parsley flakes

1 Tbsp dill weed
1 Tbsp dried salad onion
1 tsp Lawry's seasoned salt

**Instructions:**

1. Combine all ingredients and mix well.
2. Chill for at least one hour before serving. Serve with chips or fresh vegetables.

## Hot Beef Dip

*Recipe by Ona Goff*

**Ingredients:**

1 (8 oz.) package cream cheese, softened
1/2 cup sour cream
1 Tbsp milk
1/8 tsp garlic salt (or to taste)

1 (4 oz.) package dried beef, chopped (or use dried beef in a glass jar)
2 Tbsp green pepper, chopped
1 small onion, chopped
1/4 cup chopped pecans, optional

**Instructions:**

1. In a bowl, blend cream cheese, sour cream, milk, and garlic salt with a fork until smooth.
2. Add the chopped beef, green pepper, and onion, mixing well.
3. Spread mixture into a glass pie plate, top with chopped pecans if desired.
4. Bake at 350°F for 15–20 minutes, or until bubbly hot.
5. Serve immediately. (May be frozen; thaw completely before baking.)

## Crabmeat Dip

*Recipe by Cynthia Hatch*

**Ingredients:**

| | |
|---|---|
| 2 (8 oz.) packages cream cheese, softened | 1/2 cup finely chopped onion |
| 2 Tbsp butter, softened | Dash of garlic powder |
| 1 Tbsp lemon juice | 1 (6 1/2 oz.) can crabmeat, flaked |
| 1 Tbsp Worcestershire sauce | 1/2 (12 oz.) bottle Heinz chili sauce |

**Instructions:**

1. In a mixing bowl, combine the cream cheese, butter, lemon juice, Worcestershire sauce, onion, and garlic powder. Form into a flattened ball.
2. Place in the refrigerator for at least 30 minutes before serving.
3. Transfer to a large platter, pour the chili sauce over the cream cheese mixture, and sprinkle flaked crabmeat on top.
4. Serve with crackers.

## Dill Dip

*Recipe by Ona Goff*

**Ingredients:**

| | |
|---|---|
| 1 cup Hellmann's mayonnaise | 2 Tbsp minced onion |
| 1 cup sour cream | 2 Tbsp dill weed |
| 2 Tbsp parsley flakes | 2 tsp Lawry's seasoned salt |

**Instructions:**

1. Mix all ingredients well in a bowl.
2. Store in the refrigerator until ready to serve. Serve with Fritos or potato chips.

Delicious Ideas!

## Spinach Dip for Raw Vegetables

*Recipe by Mildred Buford*

### Ingredients:

1 cup mayonnaise
1 cup sour cream
1 (10 oz.) package frozen
chopped spinach, thawed and
drained

1 package Ranch Style
buttermilk dressing mix

### Instructions:

1. Squeeze excess water from the spinach.
2. In a large bowl, mix the mayonnaise and sour cream, then add the dressing mix and spinach.
3. Cover and refrigerate overnight to allow flavors to blend.

## Pimento Cheese Dip

*Recipe by Ona Goff*

### Ingredients:

1/2 cup mayonnaise
1 (2 oz.) jar pimento, drained
(reserve liquid)
2 tsp Worcestershire sauce

1 tsp prepared mustard
1 cup extra-sharp Cheddar
cheese, cubed (or use a milder
cheese)

### Instructions:

1. In a blender, combine the mayonnaise, pimento (including some reserved liquid), Worcestershire sauce, mustard, and half of the cheese. Blend until smooth.
2. Add the remaining cheese and blend until the mixture is smooth and creamy.
3. Serve with crackers or as a sandwich spread.

# Zucchini Relish

*Recipe by Julie Lange Peyton*

## Ingredients:

12 cups zucchini, chopped
4 1/2 cups onion, chopped
3 green peppers, chopped
2 red peppers, chopped
5 cups sugar

2 1/2 cups cider vinegar
1 Tbsp dry mustard
2 tsp turmeric
2 tsp celery seed
2 Tbsp mustard seed

## Instructions:

1. Place the chopped vegetables in a large bowl and cover with 1 cup pickling salt. Let stand overnight.
2. Drain and rinse with cold water, then squeeze out excess water.
3. In a large pot, combine the sugar, cider vinegar, dry mustard, turmeric, celery seed, and mustard seed.
4. Add the vegetables to the mixture, bring to a boil, and then simmer for 15 minutes.
5. Pack the relish into sterilized jars and seal. This recipe does not require a boiling water bath.

# Cranberry Relish

*Recipe by Dorothy M. Washington*

## Ingredients:

1/2 package (or 2 cups) fresh cranberries
1 orange, seeded
2 packages Knox gelatin
1/2 cup cold water

1 small package lemon Jell-O
1 1/4 cups hot water
1 small can crushed pineapple
3/4 to 1 cup chopped nuts

## Instructions:

1. Grind together the cranberries and orange, then add sugar and let sit for about 1 1/2 hours to dissolve.
2. Dissolve Knox gelatin in cold water for 5 minutes.
3. Dissolve lemon Jell-O in hot water, then stir in the gelatin.
4. Add the cranberry and orange mixture, pineapple, and nuts. Mix well.
5. Refrigerate until set. This relish can be made several days in advance.

# Food Quantities for 25, 50 & 100 Servings

| Food | 25 Servings | 50 Servings | 100 Servings |
|---|---|---|---|
| Rolls | 4 dozen | 8 dozen | 16 dozen |
| Bread | 50 slices or 3 (1-lb.) loaves | 100 slices or 6 (1-lb.) loaves | 200 slices or 12 (1-lb.) loaves |
| Butter | 1/2 pound | 3/4 to 1 pound | 1 1/2 pounds |
| Mayonnaise | 1 cup | 2 to 3 cups | 4 to 6 cups |
| Mixed Filling for Sandwiches (meat, eggs, fish) | 1 1/2 quarts | 2 1/2 - 3 quarts | 5 to 6 quarts |
| Jams & Preserves | 1 1/2 lb. | 3 lb. | 6 lb. |
| Soup | 1 1/2 gallons | 3 gallons | 6 gallons |
| Salad Dressings | 1 pint | 2 1/2 quarts | 1/2 gallon |
| Meat, Poultry, or Fish: | | | |
| - Wieners | 6 1/2 pounds | 13 pounds | 25 pounds |
| - Hamburger | 9 pounds | 18 pounds | 35 pounds |
| - Turkey or Chicken | 13 pounds | 25 to 35 pounds | 50 to 75 pounds |
| Fish, large (whole) | 13 pounds | 25 pounds | 50 pounds |
| Fish, Fillets or Steaks | 7 1/2 pounds | 15 pounds | 30 pounds |

| Salads, Casseroles, Vegetables | | | |
|---|---|---|---|
| Potato Salad | 4 1/2 quarts | 2 1/4 gallons | 4 1/2 gallons |
| Scalloped Potatoes | 4 1/2 quarts or 1 (12x20") pan | 8 1/2 quarts | 17 quarts |
| Mashed Potatoes | 9 pounds | 18 to 20 pounds | 25 to 35 pounds |
| Spaghetti | 1 1/4 gallons | 2 1/2 gallons | 5 gallons |
| Baked Beans | 3/4 gallon | 1 1/4 gallons | 2 1/2 gallons |
| Jello Salad | 3/4 gallon | 1 1/4 gallons | 2 1/2 gallons |
| Canned Vegetables | 1 #10 can | 2 1/2 #10 cans | 4 #10 cans |
| Fresh Vegetables: | | | |
| - Lettuce (for salads) | 4 heads | 8 heads | 15 heads |
| - Tomatoes | 3 to 5 pounds | 7 to 10 pounds | 14 to 20 pounds |

| Desserts | | | |
|---|---|---|---|
| Cake | 1 (10x12") sheet cake | 1 (12x20") sheet cake | 2 (12x20") sheet cakes |
| Layer Cake | 1 1/2 (10") layer cakes | 3 (10") layer cakes | 6 (10") layer cakes |

# Broccoli Soup

*Recipe by Ona Goff*

## Ingredients:

| | |
|---|---|
| 1 bunch fresh broccoli | 1/2 cup water |
| 1 can cream of chicken soup | 1/2 tsp salt |
| 3/4 cup milk | Pinch of baking soda |
| 1/4 tsp thyme | |

## Instructions:

1. Clean, wash, and cut the broccoli into small pieces, removing the tough parts of the stalk.
2. Place broccoli in a saucepan with water, salt, and baking soda. Boil, then simmer until tender. Drain, reserving the cooking liquid.
3. In another saucepan, combine the soup, thyme, salt, and 1/4 cup of the reserved liquid. Heat, then add the cooked broccoli. Serve hot with crackers.

# French Onion Soup

*Recipe by Hope Amos*

## Ingredients:

| | |
|---|---|
| 6 large yellow onions, sliced | 1/2 cup grated Gruyere cheese |
| 2 Tbsp butter | 1 cup grated Parmesan cheese |
| 1 Tbsp olive oil | French bread, cut into 1/4-inch slices |
| 6 cans beef broth | |
| 1/3 cup red port wine | Bag of grated Mozzarella cheese |
| Salt and pepper to taste | |

## Instructions:

1. Sauté onions in butter and oil until limp, then simmer for 15 minutes.
2. Add beef broth, cover, and bake at 350°F for 30 minutes.
3. Ladle into bowls, add bread slice, sprinkle with cheeses, and bake for 10 minutes at 425°F until cheese is melted and bubbly. Broil briefly if needed for browning.

Delicious Ideas!

## Creamy French Dressing

*Recipe by Ona Goff*

**Ingredients:**

1/4 cup white vinegar
1/4 cup ketchup
1/2 tsp salt
1/2 tsp dry mustard

1/2 tsp paprika
2 tsp white sugar
1/2 cup salad oil

**Instructions:**

1. Blend all ingredients except the oil in a blender or mixer.
2. Add oil slowly while blending until well combined. Adjust sweetness with extra sugar if desired.

## Zesty Salad Dressing

*Recipe by Lois Heath*

**Ingredients:**

3/4 cup Crisco oil
1/2 cup Heinz ketchup
2 Tbsp wine vinegar
1 Tbsp granulated sugar

1 tsp salt
1/2 tsp dry mustard
1 clove garlic, thinly sliced

**Instructions:**

1. Combine ingredients in a jar with a tight lid and shake well to blend.
2. Refrigerate and shake before serving. Yields 1 1/4 cups.

## Old-Fashioned Boiled Dressing

*Recipe by Ona Goff*

**Ingredients:**

2 Tbsp flour
1 tsp dry mustard
1/2 tsp salt
1/4 tsp paprika
2 Tbsp sugar
1/2 cup cold water

2 egg yolks, beaten
1/4 cup vinegar
1 Tbsp butter or margarine
1/4 cup light cream or evaporated milk

**Instructions:**

1. Combine flour, mustard, salt, paprika, and sugar in a saucepan. Stir in water, egg yolks, and vinegar.
2. Cook over low heat, stirring constantly, until thick. Add butter and cream, then chill. Thin with extra cream if too thick when serving.

## Bacon Dressing

*Recipe by Lois Heath*

**Ingredients:**

| | |
|---|---|
| 1 cup vinegar | 1 1/4 cups sugar |
| 2 cups water | 1/4 lb. bacon, fried and crumbled |
| 1/4 cup flour | 1 1/2 tsp bacon fat |

**Instructions:**

1. Combine flour, sugar, and salt with part of the water.
2. Heat vinegar and remaining water; combine with flour mixture, stirring to avoid lumps.
3. Fry bacon, drain, and add crumbled bacon and fat to dressing. Cook to desired consistency.

## Parsley Dressing

*Recipe by Ona Goff*

**Ingredients:**

| | |
|---|---|
| 1 cup fresh parsley, chopped | 1/4 cup olive oil |
| 1/4 cup chopped chives | 1/4 cup red wine vinegar |
| 1 cup sweet pickles, drained | 1/8 cup tarragon vinegar |
| 1 clove garlic | Salt and pepper to taste |

**Instructions:**

1. Finely chop chives. Grind remaining ingredients twice, reserving any juice.
2. Add olive oil and vinegars to juice, mix well, and let stand at room temperature for 24 hours before refrigerating. Great for fresh tomatoes and cucumbers.

Delicious Ideas!

## Salad Dressing

*Recipe by Doris Mooney*

**Ingredients:**

1 Tbsp. grated onion
1/3 cup catsup
1 tsp salt
1/2 tsp paprika
1/2 cup sugar

1/4 cup lemon juice
1/2 cup oil
1 tsp celery seed
1/4 cup vinegar

**Instructions:**

1. Blend all ingredients together until smooth.
2. Pour into a blender and blend until liquefied.
3. Chill before serving.

## Celery Seed Dressing

*Recipe by Lois Heath*

**Ingredients:**

1/4 cup white sugar
1 tsp dry mustard
1 ½ Tbsp lemon juice

1/2 tsp finely chopped onion
2/3 cup salad oil
1 Tbsp celery seed

**Instructions:**

1. Combine all ingredients in a blender.
2. Blend well for about 2 minutes until smooth.
3. For one quart, double the recipe, and add 2 tsp paprika if a more vibrant color is desired.

## Fruit Salad Dressing

*Recipe by Ona W. Goff*

**Ingredients:**

1/2 cup sugar
1 Tbsp flour
1 egg
1/4 cup each of lemon, orange, and pineapple juice

1/2 pint whipped cream
Miniature marshmallows
(optional)

**Instructions:**

1. Mix sugar, flour, and egg. Add juices and cook, stirring constantly until thickened.
2. Fold in whipped cream and marshmallows if desired before serving.

## Fruit Dressing

*Recipe by Ona W. Goff*

**Ingredients:**

| | |
|---|---|
| 3/4 cup granulated sugar | 3/4 cup pineapple juice |
| 1 Tbsp heaping flour | 1/4 cup vinegar |
| 2 eggs | 1/2 cup whipped topping |

**Instructions:**

1. In a bowl, mix the flour and sugar together.
2. Add eggs and beat well until smooth.
3. Gradually add the pineapple juice and vinegar, stirring until fully combined.
4. Pour the mixture into a saucepan and cook slowly over low heat, stirring constantly, until the dressing thickens.
5. Remove from heat and let it cool completely.
6. Once cooled, fold in the whipped topping.

**Yield:** Makes 1 pint.

## Watergate Salad

*Recipe by Cecil Conroy*

**Ingredients:**

| | |
|---|---|
| 1 package pistachio Jell-O instant pudding mix | 1 (9 oz.) container Cool Whip |
| 1 can crushed pineapple with juice | Optional: Cherries, mandarin oranges, or marshmallows |

**Instructions:**

1. Combine pineapple with juice and pudding mix. Fold in Cool Whip and mix well.
2. Add any optional ingredients, mix, and chill before serving.

Delicious Ideas!

## Ambrosia Salad

*Recipe by Elizabeth Greene*

### Ingredients:

1 can chunk pineapple, drained
1 can mandarin oranges, drained
1/2 bag marshmallows

1/2 bag shredded coconut
1/2 cup sour cream

### Instructions:

1. In a large bowl, combine pineapple, oranges, marshmallows, coconut, and sour cream.
2. Mix well and chill before serving.

## Pineapple Salad

*Recipe by Elizabeth Greene*

### Ingredients:

1 large can crushed pineapple, drained
1 package pistachio pudding mix

1/2 container Cool Whip
1/2 bag miniature marshmallows

### Instructions:

1. In a mixing bowl, combine drained pineapple and pistachio pudding mix.
2. Fold in Cool Whip and marshmallows until evenly mixed.
3. Chill before serving.

## Cherry "Coke" Salad

*Recipe by Lois Heath*

### Ingredients:

1 can red, sour pitted cherries (with juice and water to make 1 cup)
1 cup sugar
1 package cherry Jell-O

1 small can crushed pineapple, drained
16 oz bottle cola (cherry cola preferred)
1 cup chopped nuts

### Instructions:

1. In a saucepan, combine cherries, cherry juice, and sugar. Bring to a boil.
2. Pour over Jell-O, stirring until dissolved. Cool the mixture.
3. Add pineapple, cola, and nuts. Mix well and refrigerate until set.

4. Ideal for holiday tables or special occasions.

## Cranberry Salad

*Recipe by Cecil Conroy*

**Ingredients:**

1 lb. bag cranberries
2 large apples, cored and chopped
1 large orange (keep peel on), seeded
1/2 cup white or pink seedless grapes, halved
2 cups sugar
1 package lemon gelatin
1/2 cup boiling water
1/2 cup chopped nuts

**Instructions:**

1. Grind cranberries, apples, and orange together; add sugar and let sit for 1 1/2 hours.
2. Dissolve gelatin in boiling water and mix with cranberry mixture.
3. Add grapes and nuts, then refrigerate until firm.
4. Serve over lettuce and top with mayonnaise if desired.

## Frozen Fruit Salad

*Recipe by Polly*

**Ingredients:**

1/2 lb. miniature marshmallows
1 (No. 2) can chunk pineapple, drained
1 (No. 2) can fruit cocktail, drained
1 small jar maraschino cherries, drained
1/2 cup chopped pecans
1/2 cup whipped topping
1/2 cup salad dressing (like Miracle Whip)
2 (3 oz.) packages cream cheese, softened

**Instructions:**

1. In a large bowl, mix drained fruits, marshmallows, and pecans.
2. Blend cream cheese, whipped topping, and salad dressing until smooth; fold into fruit mixture.
3. Store in the refrigerator or freeze for longer storage. Keeps well for several weeks.

Delicious Ideas!

## Fruit Surprise

*Recipe by Margaret Singleton*

**Ingredients:**

1 cup fruit cocktail, drained
1 small container Cool Whip

1/2 box Jell-O (dry, any flavor)
1/3 cup cottage cheese

**Instructions:**

1. Combine drained fruit cocktail, dry Jell-O mix, and cottage cheese in a bowl.
2. Fold in Cool Whip, mixing well.
3. Refrigerate until chilled.

## Pistachio Salad

*Recipe by Margaret Ann Law*

**Ingredients:**

1 package pistachio instant pudding
1 medium can, crushed pineapple (with juice)

9 oz Cool Whip
1 1/2 cups miniature marshmallows
1/2 cup chopped nuts

**Instructions:**

1. Mix dry pudding mix with the pineapple and juice in a large bowl.
2. Fold in Cool Whip, then add marshmallows and nuts.
3. Chill until set.

## Marinated Tomato Salad

*Recipe by Lois Heath*

**Ingredients:**

2 medium tomatoes, thickly sliced

1/4 cup Wish-Bone Italian dressing
Salt to taste

**Instructions:**

1. Arrange tomato slices in a shallow dish, pour Italian dressing over the top, and salt as desired.
2. Chill before serving. Makes approximately 2 cups.

# Macaroni Salad

*Recipe by Eva Jordan*

**Ingredients:**

7 oz. box macaroni
1 cup Miracle Whip (or to taste)
7 slices cheese, diced

1 medium onion, diced
Candied dill pickles, diced
Salt and pepper to taste

**Instructions:**

1. Cook macaroni according to package directions. Drain, rinse in cold water, and transfer to a mixing bowl.
2. Add salt, pepper, diced onion, pickles, and cheese.
3. Mix in Miracle Whip until well combined. Sprinkle with paprika if desired and refrigerate before serving.

# Curly Macaroni Salad

*Recipe by Margaret Sipes*

**Ingredients:**

1 (8 oz.) package curly macaroni, cooked and drained
6 hard-cooked eggs, chopped
1 small onion, finely chopped
1 stalk celery, finely diced

1 1/2 cups salad dressing
1 (6 oz.) can evaporated milk
2 tsp vinegar
2 Tbsp pickle relish
1/4 cup sugar (scant)

**Instructions:**

1. Combine cooked macaroni, eggs, onions, and celery in a large bowl.
2. In a separate bowl, mix salad dressing, milk, vinegar, relish, and sugar.
3. Pour half of the dressing over the macaroni mixture, refrigerate overnight.
4. Add the remaining dressing before serving.

## Sauerkraut Salad

*Recipe by C. Hatch*

### Ingredients:

1 large can sauerkraut, rinsed and drained
1 medium can bean sprouts
1 cup chopped celery
1 cup chopped green and red peppers

1 small onion, chopped
1 tsp celery seed
1 1/4 cups sugar
1/2 cup oil
1/2 cup vinegar (wine vinegar preferred)

### Instructions:

1. Combine sauerkraut, bean sprouts, celery, peppers, onion, and celery seed in a large bowl.
2. In a small saucepan, heat sugar, oil, and vinegar until dissolved, then pour over sauerkraut mixture.
3. Marinate in the refrigerator for at least 24 hours before serving.

### SAUERKRAUT SALAD

*Recipe by Juanita Schultz*

### Ingredients:

1 cup sugar
1 tsp salt
1/4 cup salad oil
1/4 cup water
1/2 cup vinegar

1 (2 ½ oz.) can sauerkraut, drained
1 medium onion, chopped
1 green pepper, chopped
2 cups chopped celery

### Instructions:

1. In a bowl, mix together the vinegar, salt, water, oil, and sugar until well combined.
2. In a separate large bowl, combine the drained sauerkraut, chopped onion, green pepper, and celery.
3. Pour the vinegar mixture over the sauerkraut mixture, stirring to coat all ingredients.
4. Cover and refrigerate, allowing it to marinate overnight.

# Chicken Chutney Salad

*Recipe by Lillie R. Kimbro*

**Ingredients:**

2/3 cup mayonnaise
2 Tbsp lime juice
2 Tbsp chutney
1/2 tsp curry powder
1/2 tsp grated lime rind
1/4 tsp salt

2 cups diced cooked chicken
1 (8 oz.) can crushed pineapple, drained well
1 cup chopped celery
1/2 cup thinly sliced green onion
1/4 cup chopped salted peanuts

**Instructions:**

1. Combine the first six ingredients in a bowl and set aside.
2. In a separate bowl, mix the chicken, pineapple, celery, green onion, and peanuts.
3. Pour the dressing over the chicken mixture and toss gently to coat.
4. Chill for 1-2 hours before serving. Makes about 4 1/2 cups.

# Chef's Salad

*Recipe by Lizzie Owens*

**Ingredients:**

5 cups mixed salad greens
8 cherry tomatoes, halved
4 slices Swiss cheese, quartered
4 slices boiled ham, quartered

4 hard-cooked eggs, quartered
1/4 cup finely snipped green onion
1/2 cup low-calorie dressing

**Instructions:**

1. Divide greens among four bowls.
2. Top each bowl with equal portions of ham, cheese, tomatoes, eggs, and green onion.
3. Drizzle with dressing before serving. Serves 4.

Delicious Ideas!

## Tuna Fish Salad

*Recipe by Ronnie Knott*

### Ingredients:

1 large can tuna fish, drained
2-3 Tbsp salad dressing
2 large eggs, hard-cooked and chopped

2 Tbsp pickle relish
Salt and pepper to taste
Diced onion, optional

### Instructions:

1. In a bowl, mix tuna, salad dressing, eggs, relish, salt, and pepper.
2. Stir until well combined, chill before serving.

## Spinach Casserole

*Recipe by Kitty Lange*

### Ingredients:

2 boxes frozen chopped spinach, cooked and drained
6 to 8 slices stale bread, crusts removed and buttered
2 cups sharp Cheddar cheese, grated

3 eggs, beaten
1 1/2 cups milk
3 Tbsp onion, chopped
1 Tbsp lemon juice
Salt to taste

### Instructions:

1. Butter the bread slices and place them in a 2-quart casserole dish.
2. In a separate bowl, combine spinach, onion, cheese, lemon juice, and salt.
3. Beat the eggs, add milk, and mix well.
4. Pour half of the egg mixture over the bread, top with the spinach mixture, and then pour the remaining egg mixture over the top.
5. Cover and refrigerate for several hours or overnight.
6. Preheat oven to 350°F, and bake uncovered for 45 to 60 minutes until set. Serves 6-8.

## Mushroom-Potato Casserole

*Recipe by Margaret Sipes*

### Ingredients:

2 lbs. potatoes, peeled and thinly sliced
1/2 lb. fresh mushrooms, sliced
1 cup shredded Gruyere cheese
1 cup shredded Cheddar cheese
1/2 cup dry curd cottage cheese
1/2 cup sour cream

1 medium onion, finely chopped
1 tsp dried thyme
2 Tbsp flour
Salt and pepper to taste
1/4 cup wheat germ
2 Tbsp butter or margarine

### Instructions:

1. In a medium bowl, combine cheeses, sour cream, cottage cheese, onion, and thyme.
2. Butter a 2-quart baking dish and layer one-third of the potatoes on the bottom.
3. Spread half of the cheese mixture and half of the flour-tossed mushrooms over the potatoes. Season with salt and pepper.
4. Repeat layers, ending with a layer of potatoes on top. Sprinkle with wheat germ and dot with butter.
5. Cover and bake at 350°F for 1 to 1 1/4 hours, or until potatoes are tender. Let cool for 10 minutes before serving. Makes 4 servings.

## Potato Casserole

*Recipe by Lucille Place*

### Ingredients:

1 (2 lb.) package frozen hash browns, thawed
1/4 lb. margarine, melted
2 cans cream of chicken soup
1-pint sour cream

1/2 cup chopped onion
2 cups shredded sharp Cheddar cheese
2 cups crushed corn flakes or Ritz crackers

### Instructions:

1. Pour melted margarine over hash browns in a large bowl.
2. In a separate bowl, mix soup, sour cream, onions, and cheese. Add this mixture to the hash browns, stirring well.
3. Pour into a 9x13-inch baking dish. Top with crumbs and drizzle additional melted margarine over the top.
4. Bake at 350°F for 45 minutes, uncovered.

Delicious Ideas!

## Scalloped Potatoes

*Recipe by Elizabeth Greene*

**Ingredients:**

6-8 medium potatoes, peeled and
thinly sliced
3 large onions, thinly sliced
3 Tbsp flour

1 1/2 tsp pepper
2 cups milk
2 Tbsp butter or margarine

**Instructions:**

1. Preheat oven to 375°F. Parboil potatoes in salted boiling water for 3 minutes, then drain.
2. Layer potatoes and onions in a 10-cup baking dish, sprinkling flour, salt, and pepper between layers. Pour milk over the top and dot with butter.
3. Cover and bake for 45 minutes. Uncover and bake an additional 15 minutes, or until potatoes are tender and slightly browned on top.

## Corn Custard Pudding

*Recipe by Eva Jordan*

**Ingredients:**

1 (16 oz) can cream-style corn
3 eggs, beaten
3/4 cup sugar
2 Tbsp flour
Pinch of salt
Dash of black pepper

Evaporated milk (to reach
desired consistency)
1/2 stick margarine or butter,
dotted on top
Paprika, for garnish

**Instructions:**

1. Preheat oven to 350°F. In a large bowl, mix corn, beaten eggs, sugar, flour, salt, and pepper.
2. Add enough evaporated milk to reach a custard-like consistency. Pour into a 1-quart baking dish.
3. Dot with butter and sprinkle paprika over the top.
4. Place on a cookie sheet and bake for 45 minutes until set.

## Tarragon Creamed Peas

*Recipe by Ona Goff*

**Ingredients:**

1 (10 oz) package frozen peas
2 Tbsp butter or margarine
2 Tbsp flour
1 tsp salt

1/4 tsp dried tarragon
Dash of white pepper
1 1/2 cups milk

**Instructions:**

1. Cook peas according to package directions, then drain.
2. In a saucepan, melt butter and blend in flour, salt, tarragon, and pepper. Gradually stir in milk, cooking over low heat until thickened.
3. Add cooked peas, stir well, and serve hot.

## Old-Fashioned Country Greens

*Recipe by Cora Bohanna*

**Ingredients:**

3 or 4 bunches fresh turnip and
mustard greens
1/2 lb. salt pork

1 large can spinach
1 Tbsp salt
1 tsp cayenne pepper

**Instructions:**

1. Remove stems from greens and wash thoroughly. In a large pot, cook salt pork in 3-4 cups water for 45 minutes.
2. Add greens and simmer for 2 1/2 to 3 hours.
3. Season with salt and cayenne pepper during the last 45 minutes of cooking. Serve hot.

## Old-Fashioned String Beans

*Recipe by Beverly Rose*

**Ingredients:**

1 cup fresh green beans with
liquid
2 medium potatoes, diced
1/4 lb. bacon, diced

1 small onion, chopped
1 cup water
1/4 tsp salt

Delicious Ideas!

**Instructions:**

1. In a pot, brown bacon, then add green beans, potatoes, onion, water, and salt.
2. Simmer for about 30 minutes until potatoes are tender.

## Broccoli Casserole

*Recipe by Loria Bohanna Moore*

**Ingredients:**

2 boxes frozen chopped broccoli, cooked and drained
3/4 cup shredded Cheddar cheese
3/4 cup mayonnaise
2 eggs, beaten

1 can cream of celery soup
1/2 cup minced onion
4 slices bread, toasted and cut into squares

**Instructions:**

1. Preheat oven to 350°F. In a large bowl, combine broccoli, cheese, mayonnaise, eggs, soup, and onion.
2. Transfer mixture to a 2-quart baking dish and top with toasted bread squares.
3. Bake uncovered for 40 minutes until bubbly and golden.

## Broccoli and Rice Casserole

*Recipe by Margaret Sipes*

**Ingredients:**

1 cup quick-cooking rice
2 packages frozen broccoli, cooked and drained
1 (8 or 9 oz) jar Cheez Whiz

1 can cream of celery soup
1 stick butter or margarine
3/4 can water

**Instructions:**

1. Preheat oven to 350°F. Spread uncooked rice in the bottom of a casserole dish, then layer cooked broccoli over it.
2. In a saucepan, combine Cheez Whiz, soup, butter, and water, heating until blended.
3. Pour over broccoli and rice. Bake for 45 minutes or until bubbling in the center.

## Stove Top Candied Yams

*Recipe by Cora Bohanna*

**Ingredients:**

4 or 5 medium yams, peeled and quartered
1 1/2 cups white sugar

1/2 stick butter
1/4 cup water
Nutmeg, to taste

**Instructions:**

1. Place yams in a heavy saucepan, adding sugar, butter, and water.
2. Sprinkle with nutmeg and bring to a boil. Reduce heat to a simmer and cook until yams are tender, stirring occasionally. The yams will create their own syrup.

## Come and Get It Macaroni

*Recipe by Polly*

**Ingredients:**

2 cups elbow macaroni
1 (16 oz) can green peas, drained
1 (6 oz) can mushrooms, drained
1 (18 oz) can tomato juice

1 (16 oz) can tomatoes, undrained
1 envelope onion soup mix
2 (5 oz) cans diced chicken

**Instructions:**

1. In a large skillet, combine mushroom and pea liquids, tomato juice, tomatoes, and onion soup mix. Bring to a boil.
2. Gradually add macaroni and cook, covered, until tender, stirring occasionally.
3. Stir in mushrooms, peas, and diced chicken, heating through. Serve hot.

Delicious Ideas!

## MEAT COOKING GUIDE

**Cooking Methods:**

• **Sear**: High heat (350-400°F) until the exterior is dark golden brown, creating a crisp, flavorful crust. Ideal for most cuts of meat. Ensure the meat is at room temperature before cooking (remove from fridge at least 30 minutes before). Sear until a crust forms, then turn and repeat on the other side.

• **Roast**: High heat (350-425°F) in no liquid for a short time, best for tender cuts like a whole beef rib roast or chicken. Use cuts with some fat to prevent drying. Rest the meat for 20 minutes before carving.

• **Braise**: Low heat (225-250°F) in a small amount of liquid for a long time (4-12 hours), ideal for tougher cuts.

• **Stew**: Low heat (225-250°F) in a large amount of liquid for a long time (2-4 hours). Sear meat first, bring to a simmer in liquid, then add vegetables, herbs, and spices. Best for leaner, tougher cuts.

• **Grill**: High heat from smoldering embers. Ideal for flat, lean cuts as excess fat can cause flare-ups. Flip once for optimal grilling.

• **Stir Fry**: Medium-high heat. Ideal for boneless, medium-tender meat, regularly tossed. Use sesame or grape seed oil for added flavor.

∾

## Country Supper

*Recipe by Eva Jordan*

**Ingredients:**

6 slices bacon, fried until crisp
4 large potatoes, sliced
3 carrots, sliced

1 onion, sliced
1 bunch broccoli, chopped
1 lb. smoked sausage, sliced

**Instructions:**

1. Fry bacon until crisp, then remove from skillet. In the bacon drippings, sauté potatoes, carrots, onion, and broccoli until tender.
2. Add smoked sausage and heat, covered, for 12-15 minutes. Garnish with crumbled bacon. Serves 4-6

## Ivan Good

*Recipe by Lois Health*

**Ingredients:**

10 potatoes, peeled and diced
1 lb. sausage, cooked with salt, pepper, and sage, then drained
1 (16 oz) container sour cream

1 package Lipton dry onion soup mix
1/2 tsp sweet basil

**Instructions:**

1. Cook potatoes until tender, then drain.
2. Add sausage, sour cream, onion soup mix, and basil to the potatoes. Add milk to thin to soup consistency.
3. Bring to a boil, stirring constantly, then simmer for 15 minutes. Serve hot.

## Barbecued Pork Chops

*Recipe by Betty Williams*

**Ingredients:**

8 lean pork chops
1/2 cup ketchup
1/3 cup vinegar
1 cup water

1 tsp salt
1 tsp celery salt
1/2 tsp nutmeg
1 bay leaf

**Instructions:**

## Delicious Ideas!

1. Brown pork chops in hot shortening. Mix ketchup, vinegar, water, salt, celery salt, nutmeg, and bay leaf.
2. Pour mixture over chops and bake at 325°F for 1 1/2 hours, turning chops once during baking.

## Curried Spareribs

*Recipe by Irene Collier*

**Ingredients:**

3 lb. pork spareribs, cut into serving-sized pieces
2 Tbsp brown sugar
2 Tbsp prepared mustard
2 Tbsp cider vinegar

2 Tbsp water
1 tsp curry powder
1/2 tsp garlic powder
Salt to taste

**Instructions:**

1. Place ribs on a rack in a 13 x 9 x 2-inch baking pan. Cover with foil and bake at 350°F for 1 1/2 hours.
2. In a small saucepan, combine brown sugar, mustard, vinegar, water, curry powder, and garlic powder. Cook for 3 minutes.
3. Remove ribs from the oven, season with salt, brush with sauce, and bake uncovered for another 25-30 minutes.

## Sauerkraut and Spareribs

*Recipe by Irene Collier*

**Ingredients:**

| | |
|---|---|
| 2 lb. spareribs, seasoned to taste with salt and pepper | 1 apple, sliced thin |
| ¾ cup flour | 4 Tbsp. minced onion |
| 4 Tbsp. fat (for browning) | 4 Tbsp. green pepper, chopped |
| 2 (No. 2) cans sauerkraut | 1 cup water |

**Instructions:**

1. Season the spareribs with salt and pepper, then dredge them in flour.
2. In a large skillet, heat the fat and brown the floured spareribs until well-browned on all sides.
3. Remove the spareribs from the skillet and set aside.
4. In the same skillet, add the sauerkraut, apple slices, green pepper, onion, and 1 cup of water, stirring to combine.
5. Place the browned spareribs on top of the sauerkraut mixture.
6. Cover the skillet and cook over high heat until the mixture starts to bubble. Reduce to low heat and continue cooking, covered, for about 2 ½ hours, or until the spareribs are tender.

## Breakfast Casserole

*Recipe by Cynthia Hatch*

**Ingredients:**

| | |
|---|---|
| 16 slices white bread, trimmed and buttered | 8 eggs |
| 2 cups chopped ham or cooked sausage, or 1 lb. fried bacon, crumbled | 3 cups milk |
| | 1/2 tsp salt |
| 16 oz Velveeta cheese, cubed | 1/2 tsp dry mustard |
| | 2 cups crushed corn flakes |
| | 1/2 cup melted margarine |

Delicious Ideas!

**Instructions:**

1. Arrange 8 slices of buttered bread in a greased 13 x 9-inch pan, buttered side up. Top with ham and cheese, then cover with remaining bread, buttered side up.
2. In a bowl, whisk eggs, milk, salt, and mustard. Pour over bread, cover, and refrigerate overnight.
3. Remove from the fridge 1 hour before baking. Mix corn flakes and melted margarine, sprinkle over the casserole.
4. Bake at 350°F for 1 hour, uncovered.

## Creole Jambalaya

*Recipe by Barbara Jordan*

**Ingredients:**

| | |
|---|---|
| 1 Tbsp shortening | 1 clove garlic, minced |
| 1 lb. ham, cubed | 2 Tbsp chopped parsley |
| 1/2 cup chopped green pepper | 2 cups uncooked rice |
| 1 Tbsp flour | 2 Tbsp Worcestershire sauce |
| 3 cups cooked shrimp | 1 1/4 tsp salt |
| 3 cups diced tomatoes | 1/2 tsp thyme |
| 2 1/2 cups water | 1/4 tsp red pepper |
| 1 large onion, sliced | |

**Instructions:**

1. In a skillet, heat shortening and cook ham and pepper for 5 minutes. Stir in flour until smooth, then cook 1-2 minutes.
2. Add shrimp, tomatoes, water, onion, garlic, and parsley, then bring to a boil.
3. Stir in rice, Worcestershire, salt, thyme, and red pepper. Cover and cook over low heat for 30 minutes, until rice is tender and liquid is absorbed.

## Swiss Chicken and Ham Bake

*Recipe by Sis Ona W. Goff*

**Ingredients:**

1 medium onion, chopped
4 Tbsp butter
6 Tbsp flour
1 tsp salt
1/2 tsp pepper
2 cans mushrooms (do not drain)
2 cups light cream (or half-and-half)

4 Tbsp dry sherry
4 cups cubed turkey or chicken
2 cups cubed cooked ham
1 cup shredded Swiss cheese
Optional: 4 oz water chestnuts, sliced

**Instructions:**

1. In a skillet, sauté onion in butter until tender. Blend in flour, salt, and pepper.
2. Stir in undrained mushrooms, cream, and sherry, cooking until thickened.
3. Combine with turkey and ham, then transfer to a 1 1/2-quart baking dish.
4. Mix 3 cups soft breadcrumbs with 3 Tbsp melted butter and spread around the edges of the casserole.
5. Bake at 400°F for 25-35 minutes, until lightly browned.

## Rice Chinese

*Recipe by C. Hatch*

**Ingredients:**

1 lb. veal, pork, or beef, cut into 1/2-inch cubes
1 1/2 cups chopped onion
1 1/2 cups chopped celery
1 cup diced green pepper
1/2 cup instant rice

1 cup water
1 can peas, drained
3 Tbsp chopped pimiento
1 Tbsp soy sauce
1 can condensed mushroom soup
2 cups Chow Mein noodles

**Instructions:**

1. Brown meat in hot fat, then add onion, celery, and green pepper, cooking until tender.
2. Add rice, soup, water, peas, pimiento, and soy sauce. Season with salt and pepper.
3. Transfer to a 2-quart casserole and bake at 325°F for 1 1/2 hours. Add Chow Mein noodles on top for the last 5 minutes.

Delicious Ideas!

## Ricotta Rice

*Recipe by Barbara Jordan*

### Ingredients:

1 1/2 lb. diced chicken
1 lb. regular rice, presoaked for
30 minutes
3 large onions, chopped

2 sticks butter
2 large cans chicken broth
3/4 cup grated Romano cheese

### Instructions:

1. Melt one stick of butter and sauté onions lightly.
2. Add remaining butter, diced chicken, and soaked rice, cooking until rice absorbs butter.
3. Gradually add chicken broth, 2 cups at a time, until rice absorbs it.
4. Stir in Romano cheese, cover, and let sit for 15 minutes before serving.

## Chicken Divan

*Recipe by Mildred Buford*

### Ingredients:

1 box frozen broccoli spears
2 whole chicken breasts, cooked
and cubed
1 can cream of chicken soup

1/2 cup Hellmann's mayonnaise
1/2 tsp curry powder
1/2 tsp lemon juice
Dried breadcrumbs for topping

### Instructions:

1. Preheat oven to 350°F.
2. Boil broccoli in salted water until just tender; drain well.
3. In a baking dish, layer broccoli and cubed chicken.
4. In a small bowl, combine soup, mayonnaise, curry powder, and lemon juice. Pour this mixture over the broccoli and chicken.
5. Top with bread crumbs and bake until bubbly and lightly browned.

## Escalloped Chicken

*Recipe by Margaret Sipes*

**Ingredients:**

1 1/2 cups boiled chicken, diced
1 can cream of mushroom soup
1 can cream of chicken soup
1 can cream of chicken noodle
soup

1 beaten egg
6 slices white bread, toasted and
broken up

**Instructions:**

1. Preheat oven to 350°F.
2. In a large bowl, mix all soups, beaten egg, bread pieces, and diced chicken.
3. Pour mixture into a baking dish and bake for 1 hour.

## Chicken Lasagna

*Recipe by Floyd Collier*

**Ingredients:**

1 (3-3 1/2 lb.) broiled fryer
chicken, deboned and diced
1 (16 oz) package lasagna
noodles, cooked
2 celery stalks, cut in half
1 carrot, cut in half
1 medium onion, diced
1 garlic clove, minced

1 (8 oz) package mozzarella
cheese slices
2 (15 oz) cans tomato sauce
1 (10 oz) package broccoli,
cooked and chopped
1 cup grated Parmesan cheese
3 cups milk
1 1/2 sticks butter
1 cup flour

**Instructions:**

1. In a pot, cook chicken with celery, carrot, onion, garlic, and salt. Once cooked, remove chicken and refrigerate.
2. In a skillet, prepare a white sauce by melting butter and stirring in flour until smooth. Slowly add milk, stirring until thickened. Add chopped broccoli and diced chicken.
3. In a large roasting pan, layer lasagna noodles, sauce, mozzarella, and tomato sauce. Repeat layers, ending with cheese on top.
4. Cover with foil and bake at 375°F for 40 minutes.

## Chicken Cacciatore

*Recipe by Barbara Jordan*

**Ingredients:**

3-3 1/2 lb. frying chicken, cut into pieces
1/4 cup flour
1 tsp salt
1/4 tsp pepper
1/4 cup salad oil
1 3/4 cups whole peeled tomatoes with juice

2/3 cup tomato paste
3/4 cup canned mushrooms with liquid
1/2 cup water
1/2 cup chopped onion
1 crushed garlic clove
1/2 tsp Italian seasoning
1/4 tsp oregano leaves

**Instructions:**

1. Coat chicken with seasoned flour. Brown chicken in oil in a large skillet, then pour off excess fat.
2. Combine tomatoes, tomato paste, mushrooms, water, onion, garlic, Italian seasoning, and oregano. Pour over chicken.
3. Cover and simmer for 45 minutes until tender. Serve with pasta.

## Breast of Chicken with Curry Sauce

*Recipe by Myra J. Woods*

**Ingredients:**

2 poached chicken breasts, boned and halved
2 Tbsp butter
3 Tbsp flour
Salt and pepper to taste

1 Tbsp curry powder
1 1/2 cups rich chicken broth
1/2 cup heavy cream
1/4 cup chopped chutney

**Instructions:**

1. Melt butter in a saucepan and add flour, salt, pepper, and curry powder, stirring until smooth.
2. Gradually add chicken broth and cream, stirring constantly. Add chutney and bring to a simmer.
3. Place one chicken breast half on each plate, spoon sauce over, and serve with plain rice or rice with raisins and coconut.

# Teriyaki Chicken

*Recipe by Winifred Bondurant*

**Ingredients:**

3-4 boneless, cubed chicken breast halves
1/2 cup beef broth
1/2 cup chopped celery
1/2 cup chopped onion
1/2 cup diced green pepper

1 Tbsp teriyaki sauce
1/8 tsp pepper
Sliced tomatoes and mushrooms (optional)
1 tsp cornstarch, dissolved in water (optional)

**Instructions:**

1. In a skillet, brown chicken in vegetable oil.
2. Add beef broth, celery, onion, green pepper, and pepper, cooking over medium heat for 5-6 minutes.
3. Stir in teriyaki sauce, tomatoes, and mushrooms if using. Cook uncovered for 3-4 more minutes. Thicken sauce with cornstarch mixture if desired.

# Chicken In A Pot

**Ingredients:**

2 carrots, sliced
2 onions, sliced
2 celery stalks, cut into 1-inch pieces
1 (3 lb.) broiler-fryer or 4 chicken breasts

2 tsp salt
1/2 tsp coarse black pepper
1/2 cup water, chicken broth, or white wine (or 1 cup if cooking on high)
1 tsp basil

**Instructions:**

1. Place the carrots, onions, and celery in the bottom of a slow cooker.
2. Add the chicken on top of the vegetables.
3. Sprinkle with salt, pepper, and basil.
4. Pour water, broth, or wine over the chicken and vegetables.
5. Cover and cook on low for 8 to 10 hours, or on high for 3 ½ to 4 ½ hours (using 1 cup of liquid if cooking on high).

Delicious Ideas!

## Chicken a la French

*Recipe by Winifred Bondurant*

**Ingredients:**

6 boneless, skinless chicken
breast halves
6 slices mozzarella cheese
1 tomato, chopped
1/4 tsp oregano
1/4 tsp sage
3 Tbsp melted butter

1/2 tsp Worcestershire sauce
1/2 cup soft breadcrumbs
2 Tbsp parsley flakes
2 Tbsp grated Parmesan cheese
1 (7/8 oz) packet chicken gravy
mix
1 cup water

**Instructions:**

1. Pound chicken breasts until thin, then place a slice of cheese and a spoonful of tomato mixture on each. Roll up, securing with toothpicks.
2. Dip each roll in butter and coat with breadcrumbs, then bake at 350°F for 40 minutes.
3. Prepare gravy as directed, spooning some over the chicken before returning to the oven for an additional 10 minutes.

## Milanese Chicken with Parmesan Rice

*Recipe by Margaret Sipes*

**Ingredients:**

1 large broiler-fryer chicken, cut
up
1 (6 oz) envelope Italian salad
dressing mix
2 Tbsp vegetable oil
1 medium onion, cut into wedges

1 green pepper, cut into strips
1 tomato, cut into wedges
1 cup converted rice
1/2 cup dry vermouth
1 can chicken broth
2 Tbsp grated Parmesan cheese

**Instructions:**

1. Sprinkle chicken with salad dressing mix and brown in oil in a large skillet.
2. Add onion, cover, and cook on low for 25 minutes. Meanwhile, bring chicken broth to a boil, adding rice. Simmer until liquid is absorbed.
3. Remove chicken, keeping warm. Add vermouth to skillet, scraping up browned bits. Add green pepper and tomatoes; cook briefly, then serve over rice, garnished with Parmesan.

## Turkey Hash

*Recipe by Eva Jordan*

**Ingredients:**

4 cups diced cooked turkey
4-5 medium potatoes, diced
1 large yellow onion, diced

Salt and pepper to taste
1/2 cup cooking oil
1/2 cup water

**Instructions:**

1. In a heavy skillet, heat oil and sauté potatoes, onion, and turkey.
2. Season with salt and pepper, adding water to prevent sticking. Cook until potatoes are tender, adding more water if necessary.

## Steak And Potatoes

*Recipe by Anita Deel*

**Ingredients:**

2 ½ - 3 lb. round steak
Flour, for dredging
Salt and pepper, to taste
4 cups water
4 beef bouillon cubes

1 large onion, sliced ¼ inch thick
5 medium potatoes, sliced ¼ inch thick
1/4 cup shortening

**Instructions:**

1. Season flour with salt and pepper to taste. Cut steak into serving-size pieces and dredge each piece in the seasoned flour.
2. In a large skillet, heat shortening over medium heat. Sauté steak pieces in the hot fat until browned on both sides. Drain off excess fat.
3. Layer the sliced potatoes over the browned steak in the skillet. Place the onion slices on top of the potatoes.
4. Dissolve bouillon cubes in water and pour over the steak, potatoes, and onions.
5. Simmer on the stovetop until everything is very tender, or bake in a slow oven at 275°–300°F until done.

Delicious Ideas!

## My Favorite Beef Stew

*Recipe by Verlin J. Place*

### Ingredients:

2 lb. beef, cut into chunks
1/2 lb. salt pork or bacon, diced
2 Tbsp flour
1 tsp salt
1/2 tsp pepper
1 large onion, chopped
1 cup beef broth
6 medium potatoes, cut into chunks

6 carrots, cut into chunks
3 ribs celery, chopped
12 peppercorns
3 whole cloves
1/4 cup chopped parsley
1/2 bay leaf
1/2 cup sherry or dry wine

### Instructions:

1. In a Dutch oven, sauté salt pork over low heat until crisp, then brown beef in drippings. Sprinkle with flour, salt, and pepper.
2. Add onion, beef broth, peppercorns, cloves, parsley, and bay leaf. Cover and simmer for 3 hours without stirring.
3. Add sherry and cook for an additional 15 minutes.
4. Separately, cook potatoes, carrots, and celery in a small amount of water until tender, then add to stew for the last 15 minutes before serving. Serves 8.

## Pepper Steak

*Recipe by Winifred Bondurant*

### Ingredients:

1 1/2 lb. boneless chuck, cut into thin strips
1 Tbsp shortening
1 1/2 cups water
3 Tbsp soy sauce

1/2 cup Wish-Bone low-calorie Russian dressing
2 medium green peppers, cut into thin strips
2 medium onions, thinly sliced

### Instructions:

1. In a large skillet, heat shortening and brown meat.
2. Add water, Russian dressing, and soy sauce. Cover and simmer for 30 minutes.
3. Add green pepper and onions, simmering for an additional 10 minutes until tender. Serves about 6.

# Beef Stroganoff

*Recipe by Verlin J. Place*

## Ingredients:

1/4 cup butter, divided
1 1/2 tsp minced onion
2 lb. filet of beef, cut into strips
3/4 tsp salt
2 1/2 cups thinly sliced
mushrooms

Dash of nutmeg
3/4 tsp liquid brown gravy
seasoning
1 cup sour cream

## Instructions:

1. Melt 2 Tbsp butter in a skillet, add onion, and cook until golden.
2. Brown beef strips in the skillet, then set aside.
3. In the same skillet, melt remaining butter and cook mushrooms, adding nutmeg. Return beef to the skillet.
4. Blend gravy seasoning into sour cream and stir into the skillet. Heat through before serving. Yields 6 servings.

# Zucchini-Crusted Pizza

*Recipe by Julie Lange Peyton*

## Ingredients:

3 1/2 cups coarsely grated
zucchini
3 eggs, beaten
1/3 cup flour
1/2 cup grated mozzarella cheese

1/2 cup grated Parmesan cheese
1 Tbsp fresh basil, minced (or
1/2 tsp dried)
Salt and pepper to taste

## Instructions:

1. Preheat oven to 350°F. Salt grated zucchini and let sit for 15 minutes, then squeeze out excess moisture.
2. In a bowl, combine zucchini, eggs, flour, cheeses, basil, salt, and pepper.
3. Spread mixture into an oiled 9x13-inch baking pan. Bake for 20-25 minutes until the surface is firm, then brush with oil and broil under moderate heat for 5 minutes.
4. Add pizza toppings as desired, starting with pizza sauce and cheese. Bake at 350°F for 25 minutes.

# Delicious Ideas!

### Zucchini Lasagna

*Recipe by Julie Lange Peyton*

**Ingredients:**

1 1/2 medium zucchini, thinly sliced
1 Tbsp olive oil
1 lb. ground beef
2 cloves garlic, minced
1/2 cup chopped onion
1 (8 oz) can tomato sauce
1 can Italian-style tomatoes, chopped (or 2-3 large fresh tomatoes)
1/2 tsp oregano
1/4 tsp basil
1 egg
1 lb. ricotta or cottage cheese
1/2 to 1 lb. mozzarella or Swiss cheese, shredded
1/2 to 1 cup grated Parmesan cheese

**Instructions:**

1. Preheat oven to 375°F. In a skillet, heat oil and sauté beef, onion, and garlic until browned.
2. Add tomato sauce, tomatoes, oregano, and basil. Simmer for 10 minutes, stirring occasionally.
3. In a separate bowl, mix the egg with ricotta.
4. Butter or oil a 9x13-inch baking dish. Layer with zucchini slices, sprinkle with flour, then add layers of ricotta mixture, mozzarella, and meat sauce. Repeat, finishing with cheese on top.
5. Bake for 40 minutes. Let stand for 10 minutes before serving.

## Lazy Day Lasagna

*Recipe by Vi Carpenter*

**Ingredients:**

6 oz lasagna noodles
1 (15.5 oz) can spaghetti sauce
1/4 tsp oregano
1/2-1 lb. ground beef, browned and drained
1 cup cottage cheese
1 (6 oz) package sliced mozzarella cheese

**Instructions:**

1. Preheat oven to 375°F. Cook noodles according to package directions.
2. In a bowl, mix spaghetti sauce, oregano, and browned beef.
3. In a greased 10x6x1 1/2-inch baking dish, layer noodles, cottage cheese, mozzarella, and meat sauce.
4. Bake for 30 minutes until heated through. Serves 4.

## Lasagna

*Recipe by Elizabeth Greene*

### Ingredients:

8 oz medium noodles
1 1/2 lb. ground beef
1 tsp salt
1/2 tsp oregano
1/4 tsp pepper
1 (7.5 oz) can tomato sauce

1/4 tsp garlic salt
1 1/2 cups cottage cheese
1 cup sour cream
6 green onions, chopped
3/4 cup shredded Cheddar cheese
(optional)

### Instructions:

1. Preheat oven to 350°F. Cook noodles according to package directions, then drain and set aside.
2. In a skillet, brown ground beef, then add salt, oregano, pepper, tomato sauce, and garlic salt. Simmer for 5 minutes.
3. In a bowl, combine cottage cheese, sour cream, green onions, and noodles.
4. In a greased 2-quart casserole dish, layer noodle mixture and meat sauce. Top with Cheddar cheese if desired.
5. Bake for 50-60 minutes or until heated through. Serves 6.

## Tasty Hamburgers

*Recipe by Verlin J Place*

### Ingredients:

1 lb. ground beef
1 Tbsp flour

1 can Campbell's onion soup

### Instructions:

1. In a skillet, cook ground beef until done. Stir in flour and cook until thickened.
2. Add onion soup and heat through. Serve on buns or as an open-faced sandwich. Tastes similar to White Castle burgers.

Delicious Ideas!

## Cowboy Beans

*Recipe by Winifred Bondurant*

### Ingredients:

| | |
|---|---|
| 1 lb. ground beef | 1 cup ketchup |
| 2 cups chopped onion | 2 Tbsp prepared mustard |
| 2 (16 oz) cans pork and beans | 2 tsp vinegar |
| 1 (15.5 oz) can kidney beans | 1 tsp salt |

### Instructions:

1. Brown ground beef and onions in a skillet, then drain.
2. In a 2-quart casserole dish, combine beef mixture with remaining ingredients.
3. Bake at 400°F for 30 minutes.

## Cabbage Rolls

*Recipe by Vi Carpenter*

### Ingredients:

| | |
|---|---|
| 1/2 lb. ground beef | 1 egg |
| 1/2 lb. ground pork | 1 large head cabbage |
| 2 tsp salt | 1 small can tomato puree |
| 1 tsp paprika | 1 large onion, chopped |
| 1/2 tsp black pepper | 2 Tbsp fat |
| 1/2 cup rice, uncooked | 1 clove garlic (optional) |

### Instructions:

1. Place cabbage in boiling water, then remove wilted leaves. Sauté chopped onion in fat.
2. In a bowl, combine ground meats, egg, seasonings, and rice. Place a spoonful of meat mixture in each cabbage leaf and roll.
3. Place rolls in a pot, cover with tomato puree and enough water to cover. Cook over low heat for 1 hour or until rice is tender.

## Potato Puff Casserole

*Recipe by Verlin J Place*

### Ingredients:

1 lb. ground beef
1/3 cup chopped onion
1/3 cup chopped green pepper
1 Tbsp chili sauce or ketchup

1 (10 3/4 oz) can cream of mushroom soup
1/4 cup water
1 (10 oz) package frozen potato puffs

### Instructions:

1. In a skillet, cook ground beef, onion, and green pepper until beef is browned.
2. Stir in chili sauce, mushroom soup, and water. Pour mixture into a 1 1/2-quart casserole.
3. Arrange potato puffs on top and bake uncovered at 375°F for 35 minutes or until golden brown. Makes 4 servings.

## Jonni Marzetti

*Recipe by Vi Carpenter*

### Ingredients:

1 1/2-2 lb. ground beef
1 package Lipton onion soup
1 large can tomatoes, cut into chunks

3 cups cooked macaroni
Parmesan cheese
Shredded mozzarella or Romano cheese

### Instructions:

1. In a skillet, brown ground beef, then add onion soup mix and tomatoes. Cook until it begins to simmer.
2. Pour beef mixture over cooked macaroni in a baking dish. Top with Parmesan and other cheese.
3. Bake in a preheated oven for 15-20 minutes or until cheese is melted. Serve with garlic bread or rolls.

## Easy Spaghetti Sauce

*Recipe by Winifred Bondurant*

**Ingredients:**

1/2 cup chopped onion
1/4 cup chopped green pepper
1 garlic clove, crushed
2 Tbsp salad oil
1 1/4 cups water
2 cups (two 8 oz cans) tomato sauce

2/3 cup (6 oz can) tomato paste
1/2 tsp crushed oregano leaves
1/4 tsp crushed basil leaves
1 bay leaf
1 tsp sugar
1/2 tsp salt
1/8 tsp pepper

**Instructions:**

1. In a medium saucepan, sauté onion, green pepper, and garlic in oil.
2. Stir in water, tomato sauce, tomato paste, oregano, basil, bay leaf, sugar, salt, and pepper.
3. Bring to a boil, then reduce heat and simmer uncovered for 30 minutes. Remove bay leaf before serving.
4. Serve over hot, cooked spaghetti. For added flavor, add browned ground beef or sausage. Makes about 4 cups.

## Salmon Croquettes

*Recipe by Myra J. Woods*

**Ingredients:**

2 cans salmon, drained
1 can tuna, drained
2 eggs
1/2 cup chopped onion
1/2 cup chopped green pepper

1 tsp flour
5 Tbsp vegetable oil
1 cup flour mixed with 1 cup yellow cornmeal for coating

**Instructions:**

1. In a bowl, combine salmon, tuna, eggs, onion, green pepper, and 1 tsp flour.
2. Heat oil in a frying pan over medium heat.
3. Form mixture into patties, coat with flour and cornmeal mixture, and fry in hot oil until golden brown on both sides. Drain on paper towels and serve.

## Salmon Pie

*Recipe by Winifred Bondurant*

**Ingredients:**

1 large can salmon, drained
(reserve 2 Tbsp liquid)
1 Tbsp grated onion

1/4 lb. sharp cheese, grated
1/3 can cream of celery soup

**Crust:**

1 cup flour
1 1/2 tsp baking powder
1/2 tsp salt

3 Tbsp shortening
1 egg
1/4 cup milk

**Instructions:**

1. Preheat oven to 375°F. For the crust, mix flour, baking powder, salt, and shortening until crumbly. Add beaten egg and milk to form dough; knead lightly and roll out.
2. Place drained salmon in a 9-inch pie pan, top with onion, reserved salmon liquid, cheese, and 1/3 can of celery soup.
3. Place crust on top, cutting a small square in the center. Bake for 25-30 minutes, until golden. Serve with remaining soup mixed with 1/4 cup milk.

## Salmon Casserole

*Recipe by Gertrude Sampson*

**Ingredients:**

1 (16 oz) can peas, drained
1 (16 oz) can salmon, drained
and flaked

4-6 hard-boiled eggs, sliced
6 crackers, crushed

**Thin Sauce:**

1 Tbsp butter, melted
4 Tbsp flour

1 1/2 cups milk
Dash of pepper

**Instructions:**

1. Preheat oven to 375°F. In a casserole dish, layer half of the salmon, half of the eggs, and half of the peas.
2. Repeat with remaining salmon, eggs, and peas, then sprinkle crushed crackers on top.

3. For the sauce, melt butter in a saucepan, stir in flour, then add milk and pepper, stirring until thickened.
4. Pour sauce over casserole and bake for 30 minutes.

## Tuna Casserole

*Recipe by Winifred Bondurant*

**Ingredients:**

1 (10 1/2 oz) can cream of mushroom soup
1 (6 1/2 oz) can tuna, drained
1 (3 oz) can sliced mushrooms, drained

1/4 cup chopped pimiento (optional)
1 (6 oz) can evaporated milk
1 (4 oz) can chow mein noodles, divided

**Instructions:**

1. Preheat oven to 375°F.
2. In a bowl, mix soup, tuna, mushrooms, pimiento, and evaporated milk.
3. Stir in all but 1 cup of the chow mein noodles, then pour mixture into a 1 1/2-quart casserole.
4. Top with remaining chow mein noodles and bake for 25 minutes or until hot and bubbly. Serves 4-6.

## Tuna Macaroni and Cheese Casserole

*Recipe by Gertrude Sampson*

**Ingredients:**

1 (7 oz) package Kraft macaroni and cheese
1 (6 oz) can tuna, drained
1/2 cup sliced green pepper
1/2 cup chopped onion

1 cup milk
2 Tbsp salad dressing
Dash of salt and pepper
8 oz grated cheese (optional)

**Instructions:**

1. Prepare macaroni and cheese according to package directions.
2. Stir in tuna, salad dressing, green pepper, and onion. Season with salt and pepper.
3. Pour into a greased baking dish, top with extra cheese if desired, and bake at 375°F for 45 minutes.

# Fish 'N Rice for Four

*Recipe by Winifred Bondurant*

## Ingredients:

1 1/2 cups quick-cooking rice
1 1/2 cups boiling water
1/4 cup shredded carrot
1/4 cup thinly sliced celery
2 Tbsp butter or margarine
1 1/2 tsp instant chicken bouillon

Grated peel of 1 lemon
1/4 tsp poultry seasoning
4 fillets sole or other white fish
(1 lb.)
Juice of 1/2 lemon
Paprika and salt to taste

## Instructions:

1. In a 12 x 8 x 2-inch baking dish, combine rice, carrot, celery, 1 Tbsp butter, bouillon, lemon peel, and poultry seasoning. Stir in boiling water, cover with foil, and bake at 400°F for 5 minutes.
2. Remove foil, stir, and arrange fish over rice. Sprinkle with lemon juice, paprika, salt, and dot with remaining butter.
3. Cover and bake for 25 minutes until fish flakes easily. Garnish with lemon wedges and parsley if desired.

# Fried Fish a la Margherita

*Recipe by Winifred Bondurant*

## Ingredients:

2 lb. sole, flounder, or ocean perch
1 (15 oz) can tomato sauce
2 Tbsp parsley, chopped

1 tsp oregano
1/4 cup oil
1/4 cup butter

## Instructions:

1. In a small bowl, mix tomato sauce, parsley, and oregano.
2. In a skillet, heat butter and oil. Cook fish fillets 2-3 minutes on each side until golden brown.
3. Pour tomato sauce mixture over fish, simmer for 2 minutes, and serve with sauce.

## Cheesy Macaroni

*Recipe by Elizabeth Greene*

**Ingredients:**

| | |
|---|---|
| 2 cups macaroni | 4 Tbsp margarine |
| 4 1/2 cups grated Velveeta cheese | 1 beaten egg |
| | 2 tsp pepper |
| 3/4 cup evaporated milk | 1 1/2 tsp salt |

**Instructions:**

1. Preheat oven to 375°F. Cook macaroni until tender, then drain.
2. In a casserole dish, combine cooked macaroni, salt, pepper, and margarine. Stir in 4 cups of cheese.
3. Add beaten egg and pour evaporated milk over the top. Sprinkle remaining cheese on top.
4. Bake for 15-20 minutes or until bubbly and golden brown.

## Macaroni Cheese Casserole

*Recipe by Elizabeth Greene*

**Ingredients:**

| | |
|---|---|
| 2 cups uncooked macaroni | 1 tsp salt |
| 1/2 cup butter or margarine | 1/4 tsp pepper |
| 2 Tbsp flour | 1 cup grated Cheddar cheese |
| 1 1/2 cups milk | |

**Instructions:**

1. Preheat oven to 350°F. Boil macaroni in salted water for 6-8 minutes, then drain and rinse in cold water.
2. In a saucepan, melt butter, stir in flour, then gradually add milk, salt, and pepper. Cook until thickened.
3. Combine macaroni with sauce in a casserole dish. Top with grated cheese and sprinkle with paprika.
4. Bake until heated through and bubbly.

This collection of recipes completes the guide with cozy, classic dishes perfect for family meals and gatherings. From hearty casseroles and cheesy bakes to flavorful fish and seafood recipes, each offers a comforting, satisfying option that's easy to prepare.

# BREAD, ROLLS, PASTRIES

## Equivalent Measurements

| | | | |
|---|---|---|---|
| 3 teaspoons | 1 Tablespoon | 2 pints | 1 quart |
| 2 Tablespoons | 1/8 cup | 1 quart | 4 cups |
| 4 Tablespoons | 1/4 cup | 5/8 cup | 1/2 cup + 2 Tbsp |
| 8 Tablespoons | 1/2 cup | 7/8 cup | 3/4 cup + 2 Tbsp |
| 16 Tablespoons | 1 cup | 1 jigger | 1 1/2 fl. oz (3 Tbsp) |
| 8 ounces | 1 cup | 2 cups fat | 1 pound |
| 16 ounces | 1 pound | 1 pound butter | 2 cups or 4 sticks |
| 1 ounce | 2 Tbsp fat or liquid | 2 cups sugar | 1 pound |
| 2 cups | 1 pint | 4 oz uncooked macaroni | 2 1/4 cups cooked macaroni |
| 8-10 egg whites | 1 cup | 28 saltine crackers | 1 cup crumbs |
| 12-14 egg yolks | 1 cup | 4 slices bread | 1 cup crumbs |
| 1 lemon | 3 Tbsp juice | 14 square graham crackers | 1 cup crumbs |
| 1 orange | 1/3 cup juice | 22 vanilla wafers | 1 cup crumbs |

## Substitutions For Missing Ingredients

- **1 Tbsp cornstarch (for thickening)** = 2 Tbsp flour
- **1 cup sifted all-purpose flour** = 1 cup plus 2 Tbsp sifted cake flour
- **1 teaspoon baking powder** = 1/4 teaspoon baking soda plus 1/2 teaspoon cream of tartar
- **1 cup sweet milk** = 1 cup sour milk or buttermilk plus 1/2 teaspoon baking soda
- **1 cup sour milk** = 1 cup sweet milk with 1 tablespoon vinegar or lemon juice stirred in (let stand for 5 minutes)
- **3/4 cup cracker crumbs** = 1 cup breadcrumbs
- **1 teaspoon dried herbs** = 1 tablespoon fresh herbs
- **1/2 cup evaporated milk and 1/2 cup water** or **1 cup reconstituted nonfat dry milk plus 1 tablespoon butter** = 1 cup whole milk
- **1 tablespoon instant minced onion, rehydrated** = 1 small fresh onion
- **1 tablespoon prepared mustard** = 1 teaspoon dry mustard
- **1/8 teaspoon garlic powder** = 1 small pressed clove of garlic
- **1 lb. whole dates** = 1 1/2 cups pitted and cut
- **3 medium bananas** = 1 cup mashed
- **10 miniature marshmallows** = 1 large marshmallow

## Finnish Pancakes (From Finland)

*Recipe by Ona W. Goff*

**Ingredients:**

- 3/4 cup flour
- 1 Tbsp sugar
- 1 1/4 cup milk
- 2 eggs
- 1/2 stick butter

**Instructions:**

1. Preheat oven to 425°F. Melt butter in a cookie sheet with 1-inch sides.
2. In a bowl, mix flour, sugar, milk, and eggs until combined (mixture may be slightly lumpy).
3. Pour the batter into the hot melted butter in the pan.
4. Bake for 20-25 minutes or until lightly browned. Tilt pan as needed so the batter covers the pan evenly.

## Kentucky Biscuits

*Recipe by Ona W. Goff*

**Ingredients:**

- 1 1/2 cups flour
- 1 Tbsp baking powder
- 1 Tbsp sugar
- 1 tsp salt
- 1/3 cup softened lard or shortening
- 1/2 cup milk

**Instructions:**

1. Preheat oven to 450°F.
2. In a bowl, stir together flour, baking powder, sugar, and salt.
3. Make a well in the center, add milk and lard, and mix with a fork until just combined.
4. On a lightly floured surface, knead dough 6-8 times, then pat out to 1/2 inch thickness.
5. Cut into 1 3/4-inch rounds and place on an ungreased baking sheet.
6. Bake for 10-12 minutes or until golden brown. Makes 13-14 biscuits.

## Corn Bread

*Recipe by Ona W. Goff*

**Ingredients:**

- 1/2 cake yeast or 1 tsp dry yeast
- 1/4 cup lukewarm water
- 1/2 cup cornmeal
- 1 3/4 cup boiling water
- 1 1/2 tsp salt
- 2 Tbsp honey
- 1 Tbsp shortening
- 1/3 cup sourdough starter (optional)
- 1 egg, beaten
- 2 3/4 to 3 cups sifted flour

**Instructions:**

1. Soften yeast in lukewarm water.
2. Cook cornmeal in boiling water for 10 minutes. Add salt, honey, and shortening; cool slightly.
3. Stir in sourdough and egg. When mixture reaches lukewarm temperature, add yeast.
4. Gradually add flour, mixing until smooth.
5. Knead dough on a floured surface, using as little extra flour as possible, and place in a greased bowl.
6. Cover and let rise until doubled. Punch down, let rise again, then shape into loaves.
7. Place in two greased 8 1/2 x 4 1/2 x 2 1/2 inch pans, let rise again until almost doubled.
8. Bake at 425°F for 35 minutes.

## Zucchini Bread

*Recipe by Snobia Mitchell*

**Ingredients:**

- 3 eggs
- 2 cups sugar
- 1 cup oil
- 3 cups flour
- 1 tsp baking soda
- 1/2 tsp baking powder
- 1 tsp salt
- 2 tsp cinnamon
- 2 cups grated zucchini
- 1/2 cup chopped nuts
- 3 tsp vanilla

**Instructions:**

1. Preheat oven to 350°F.
2. In a large bowl, mix all ingredients in order.
3. Pour batter into two greased and floured loaf pans.
4. Bake for 1 hour. Makes 2 loaves.

## Banana Bread

*Recipe by Lois Heath*

**Ingredients:**

- 3 large bananas, mashed
- 1 cup sugar
- 2 well-beaten eggs
- 2 cups sifted flour
- 1 tsp baking soda
- 1/2 tsp salt
- 1/2 cup melted shortening
- 1 cup chopped walnuts

**Instructions:**

1. Preheat oven to 300°F.
2. In a mixing bowl, combine ingredients in order given. Let batter stand 10 minutes before pouring into the pan.
3. Bake for 45 minutes at 300°F, then reduce heat to 275°F and bake for another 45 minutes.

## Cheese Cloverleafs

*Recipe by Ona W. Goff*

**Ingredients:**

- 2 cups flour
- 4 tsp baking powder
- 1 tsp salt
- 1/4 cup butter
- 3/4 cup sharp grated cheese
- 1 egg
- 2/3 cup milk

**Instructions:**

1. Preheat oven to 400°F.
2. Sift flour, baking powder, and salt twice.
3. Work in butter using fingertips, then add cheese and mix.
4. Combine beaten egg and milk, then add to dry ingredients.

5. Portion dough into greased muffin cups and bake for 20 minutes.

## Bran Muffins

*Recipe by Cheri Morall*

**Ingredients:**

- 1 1/4 cups all-purpose flour
- 1 Tbsp baking powder
- 1/2 tsp salt
- 1/2 cup sugar
- 1 1/2 cups All-Bran cereal
- 1 1/4 cups milk
- 1 egg
- 1/3 cup shortening or vegetable oil

**Instructions:**

1. Preheat oven to 400°F. Grease muffin pan.
2. In a bowl, combine flour, baking powder, salt, and sugar.
3. Mix cereal and milk in another bowl and let stand until softened.
4. Add egg and shortening to cereal mixture, then fold in flour mixture.
5. Spoon into muffin cups and bake for 25 minutes. Makes 12 muffins.

## Pumpkin Bread

*Recipe by Mary Morall*

**Ingredients:**

- 1 cup granulated sugar
- 1/2 cup brown sugar
- 1 cup cooked or canned pumpkin
- 1/2 cup salad oil
- 2 eggs
- 2 cups sifted flour
- 1 tsp baking soda
- 1/2 tsp salt
- 1/2 tsp nutmeg
- 1/2 tsp cinnamon
- 1/4 tsp ginger
- 1/2 cup chopped nuts
- 1 cup raisins
- 1/4 cup water

**Instructions:**

1. Preheat oven to 350°F.
2. In a mixing bowl, combine sugar, pumpkin, oil, and eggs. Beat until blended.

3. Add flour, baking soda, salt, and spices; mix well.
4. Stir in nuts, raisins, and water. Pour into a greased loaf pan or Bundt pan.
5. Bake for 65 minutes or until a toothpick inserted comes out clean.

## Hushpuppies

**Ingredients:**

- 1 can white cornmeal
- 1/2 cup flour
- 1 1/2 tsp baking powder
- 3/4 tsp salt
- 2 Tbsp minced onion
- 1 egg
- 2/3 cup milk

**Instructions:**

1. Preheat oil in deep fryer to 370°F.
2. Sift together cornmeal, flour, baking powder, and salt. Stir in minced onion.
3. In another bowl, beat egg and milk, then add to dry ingredients.
4. Drop by teaspoonfuls into hot oil. Fry until golden brown.
5. Drain on paper towels. Makes about 48 hushpuppies.

## Casserole Bread

*Recipe by Ida Clemons*

**Ingredients:**

- 1 cup milk
- 3 Tbsp sugar
- 1 Tbsp butter or margarine
- 1 tsp salt
- 2 pkg dry yeast
- 1/2 cup warm water
- 4 1/2 cups sifted flour

**Instructions:**

1. Scald milk and stir in sugar, salt, and butter until melted. Let cool to lukewarm.
2. Dissolve yeast in warm water, then combine with milk mixture.
3. Gradually add flour, beating until smooth.
4. Cover and let rise for 45 minutes or until doubled in bulk.
5. Punch down and spoon into a greased 1 1/2-quart casserole. Bake at 375°F for 50-55 minutes.

## Casserole Poppy Seed Bread

*Recipe by Ona W. Goff*

### Ingredients:

- 1 cup milk
- 3 Tbsp sugar
- 1 Tbsp salt
- 1 1/2 tsp shortening
- 2 pkg dry yeast (or compressed cakes)

- 1 cup warm water
- 4 1/2 cups sifted enriched flour
- 1 egg yolk
- 1 Tbsp poppy seed

### Instructions:

1. Scald milk*, add sugar, salt, and shortening, then cool to lukewarm.
2. In a separate bowl, dissolve yeast in warm water.
3. Combine lukewarm milk mixture with dissolved yeast, then add flour. Mix until well blended.
4. Cover and let rise in a warm place until tripled in bulk, about 40 minutes.
5. Stir dough down and beat vigorously for 1/2 minute. Turn into a greased casserole.
6. Brush top with egg yolk (diluted with a little water) and sprinkle with poppy seeds.
7. Bake at 375°F for about 1 hour.

## Sourdough Starter

*Recipe by Ona W. Goff*

### Ingredients:

- 1 package dry yeast
- 2 cups flour

- 1 Tbsp sugar
- 2 cups warm water

### Instructions:

1. In a crockery or glass bowl, mix yeast, flour, sugar, and warm water. Stir to combine.

---

* How to Scald Milk - Start by pouring the milk into a saucepan on the stove. Then heat the milk over medium-low heat, which will prevent it from burning or sticking to the bottom of the pan. Keep stirring the milk for 4-5 minutes. When you notice steam and bubbles forming near the edge of the pan, take the milk off the stove.

2. Cover with cheesecloth or a loose lid and let sit at room temperature for 5 days, stirring morning and evening.
3. After 5 days, refrigerate the starter. Replenish after each use by adding equal parts flour and water, letting it sit at room temperature for 24 hours before refrigerating.

## Dumplings

*Recipe by Louise Voorhies*

**Ingredients:**

- 3/4 cup sifted flour
- 2 1/2 tsp baking powder
- 1/2 tsp salt
- 1 egg
- 1/2 cup milk

**Instructions:**

1. In a bowl, sift together flour, baking powder, and salt.
2. Beat the egg and add milk; stir into the flour mixture until just combined.
3. Drop small spoonfuls into simmering broth or stew.
4. Cover tightly and cook over low heat without lifting the cover for 15 minutes. Dumplings should be fluffy and cooked through.

## Chicken Pot Pie Dough

*Recipe by Ona W. Goff*

**Ingredients:**

- 2 cups flour
- 1 Tbsp baking powder
- 1/2 tsp salt
- 2 Tbsp shortening
- 1 egg, beaten
- 1/3 cup water

**Instructions:**

1. In a large bowl, sift together flour, baking powder, and salt.
2. Cut in shortening until the mixture resembles coarse crumbs.
3. In a separate bowl, beat egg and water together, then add to the flour mixture.
4. Roll out dough thinly on a floured surface and cut into 2-inch squares.
5. Let squares rest for 30 minutes before adding to boiling broth, one at a time.
6. Cook for about 20 minutes at a slow boil with the pan covered.

## Sarah's Dressing

*Recipe by Sarah W. Huff*

**Ingredients:**

- 1 large loaf of bread, toasted
- 2 medium onions, diced
- 1 garlic clove, minced
- 3 stalks of celery, diced
- 1/2 cup chestnuts, chopped
- 3 medium apples, diced
- 1 large mango, diced
- 1 tsp parsley
- Dash of red pepper
- Small can of chicken broth
- 2 eggs
- 1/2 stick butter
- Salt and pepper to taste

**Instructions:**

1. In a large mixing bowl, combine diced onions, garlic, celery, chestnuts, apples, mango, parsley, and red pepper with toasted bread pieces.
2. Add chicken broth, eggs, and melted butter, then season with salt and pepper to taste.
3. Mix well and stuff inside the turkey or chicken before roasting.

## Corn Bread Dressing

*Recipe by Kimberly Strain*

**Ingredients:**

- 1 small pan of baked cornbread, crumbled
- 1 package Stove Top stuffing mix
- 2 cans cream of chicken soup
- 1/2 cup chopped celery
- 1/2 cup chopped onions
- 1/2 cup chopped bell pepper
- 1 stick margarine
- Chicken broth (quantity depends on desired texture)
- 2 dashes of sage

**Instructions:**

1. In a large pot, cook chicken parts (such as necks, backs, and gizzards) in water to make broth. Remove chicken parts when tender and chop finely.
2. In the same pot, add celery, onions, bell pepper, and margarine to the broth; cook until vegetables are tender.
3. In a large bowl, combine cornbread, Stove Top stuffing, chopped chicken, cooked vegetables, and cream of chicken soup.
4. Gradually add broth until the mixture reaches a desired consistency.
5. Place dressing in a baking dish and bake at 350°F for 45-55 minutes.

# Homemade Rolls

*Recipe by Eva Jordan*

**Ingredients:**

- 5 cups flour
- 1/2 cup sugar
- 1 Tbsp salt
- 1/2 stick margarine
- 1 egg
- 1 package dry yeast

**Instructions:**

1. In a large bowl, mix flour, sugar, salt, and margarine until crumbly.
2. Add egg and 1 cup of warm water with dissolved yeast, mixing into the dry ingredients.
3. Gradually add warm water as needed to form a smooth dough.
4. Turn dough onto a floured surface and knead until tough and elastic. Place in a greased bowl, cover, and let rise in a warm place until doubled.
5. Punch down the dough, shape into tennis-ball-sized rolls, and place in a greased pan.
6. Let rise again until doubled, then bake at 350°F for 30-45 minutes.
7. Brush tops with melted margarine before serving.

# Blackberry Cobbler

*Recipe by Gertrude Sampson*

**Ingredients:**

- 2 to 3 cans blackberries
- 2 tsp lemon juice
- 1 Tbsp flour
- 1 tsp cinnamon
- 3 to 4 Tbsp sugar
- 1 to 1 1/2 sticks butter

## Delicious Ideas!

**Crust:**

- 2 cups flour
- 2/3 cup shortening
- 1 tsp salt
- 4-6 Tbsp cold water

**Instructions:**

1. Preheat oven to 350°F.
2. In a bowl, mix blackberries with lemon juice, flour, cinnamon, and sugar. Pour into an unbaked pie crust and dot with butter.
3. For the crust, combine flour, shortening, and salt. Add cold water a tablespoon at a time, mixing until dough forms.
4. Roll out dough to cover the blackberry mixture and crimp edges.
5. Bake for 45 minutes or until crust is golden brown.

# Old-Fashioned Apple Cobbler

*Recipe by Cora Bohanna*

**Ingredients:**

**Filling:**

- 3 lb. cooking apples, peeled, cored, and sliced
- 2 1/2 to 3 cups sugar
- 1/2 cup flour
- 1 Tbsp salt
- 1 1/2 sticks butter, sliced
- 3 tsp nutmeg
- 1/2 cup water

**Crust:**

- 3 1/2 cups flour
- 1 1/2 cup shortening
- 1 tsp salt
- 1/2 cup water

**Instructions:**

1. Preheat oven to 450°F.
2. In a large bowl, mix sliced apples with sugar, flour, salt, and nutmeg.
3. Transfer apple mixture to a deep baking dish and dot with butter slices. Pour water over the apple filling.
4. For the crust, mix flour, salt, and shortening until crumbly. Add water gradually to form a soft dough.
5. Roll out dough to fit over the apples, fold over the edges to cover.

6. Bake at 450°F for 30 minutes, then reduce heat to 350°F and bake for an additional 1 hour.

## Pecan Pie

*Recipe by Gail Morall*

**Ingredients:**

- 3 eggs
- 1/2 tsp salt
- 2/3 cup sugar

- 1/3 cup melted butter
- 1 cup dark corn syrup
- 1 cup pecan halves

**Instructions:**

1. Preheat oven to 375°F.
2. In a bowl, beat eggs, then add salt, sugar, melted butter, and corn syrup. Mix well.
3. Pour mixture into a prepared pie crust, sprinkle pecan halves evenly over the filling.
4. Bake for 40 minutes or until set.

## Egg Custard Pie

*Recipe by Louise James*

**Ingredients:**

- 4 eggs
- 1 cup sugar
- 2/3 cup evaporated milk

- 1/3 cup melted butter
- 1/2 tsp nutmeg
- 1/2 tsp vanilla extract

**Instructions:**

1. Preheat oven to 375°F.
2. In a mixing bowl, beat eggs and sugar until combined.
3. Stir in evaporated milk, melted butter, nutmeg, and vanilla extract, mixing until smooth.
4. Pour into a prepared pie shell and bake for 45 minutes or until a knife inserted in the center comes out clean.

Delicious Ideas!

## Sweet Potato Pie

*Recipe by Mary Frances Terry*

**Ingredients:**

- 5 large yams or sweet potatoes
- 1/2 lb. butter
- 2 cups sugar
- 7 eggs
- 1 tsp ginger
- 3 tsp cinnamon
- 1 tsp nutmeg
- 1 can evaporated milk
- 1/2 tsp salt

**Instructions:**

1. Preheat oven to 350°F. Boil yams until tender, then peel and mash with butter.
2. In a large bowl, mix mashed yams with sugar, eggs, ginger, cinnamon, nutmeg, evaporated milk, and salt.
3. Pour filling into pie shells and bake for 1 hour, or until filling is set.

## Sweet Potato Pie Filling

*Recipe by Rosella Williams*

**Ingredients**

- 4 large, sweet potatoes (yams recommended for best pie)
- 3 eggs
- 1/2 lb. creamy butter
- 1 can Carnation milk
- 1 Tbsp allspice
- 1 Tbsp vanilla flavor

**Instructions**

1. Boil sweet potatoes until tender.
2. In a saucepan, mix eggs, butter, Carnation milk, allspice, and vanilla with the sweet potatoes until smooth.
3. Pour mixture into an unbaked pie crust.
4. Bake at 300°F until set.

# Magic Pumpkin Pie Filling

*Recipe by Rosella Williams*

## Ingredients:

- 1 large can pumpkin
- 1 cup granulated sugar
- 1/2 cup brown sugar
- 1/2 lb. creamy butter
- 1/2 cup syrup
- 1 1/2 cups milk
- 1 Tbsp allspice
- A touch of honey

## Instructions:

1. In a saucepan over medium heat, mix pumpkin, granulated and brown sugar, butter, syrup, milk, allspice, and honey. Stir constantly until thickened, about 5 minutes.
2. Cool mixture and pour into a prepared pie crust. Refrigerate for several hours before serving.
3. Serve with whipped cream if desired.

# Butterscotch Pecan Pie

*Recipe by Icie Mayes*

## Ingredients

- 1 (12 oz.) pkg. butterscotch pieces
- 4 eggs
- 1 cup dark corn syrup
- 1/2 tsp. salt
- 1 cup pecan halves

## Instructions

1. Melt the butterscotch pieces and set aside.
2. In a large bowl, combine eggs, syrup, and salt. Gradually add melted butterscotch, beating until smooth.
3. Stir in pecans and pour into a pre-baked pie shell.
4. Bake at 350°F for 50 minutes or until filling is set.

# Delicious Ideas!

## Lemon Pie

*Recipe by Eva Jordan*

### Ingredients

- 1 cup sugar
- 3 Tbsp cornstarch
- 1 cup boiling water
- 4 egg yolks, slightly beaten
- 2 Tbsp butter
- 4 Tbsp lemon juice
- Grated rind of 1 lemon
- Pinch of salt
- 3 egg whites for meringue
- 2 Tbsp sugar for meringue

### Instructions

1. Mix cornstarch and sugar; gradually add boiling water, stirring until smooth.
2. Add egg yolks, butter, lemon rind, lemon juice, and salt. Cook for 2–3 minutes until thickened.
3. Pour into a baked pie shell.
4. To make meringue, beat egg whites until stiff and gradually add 2 tablespoons sugar.
5. Spread meringue on top of pie and bake in a slow oven until golden brown.

## Lemon Sponge Pie

*Recipe by Eva Jordan*

### Ingredients

- 3 Tbsp softened butter or margarine
- 1 1/4 cup sugar
- 4 eggs, separated
- 3 Tbsp flour
- Dash of salt
- 1 1/4 cup milk
- Grated peel of 2 lemons
- 1/3 cup lemon juice
- 1 (9-inch) unbaked pie shell

### Instructions

1. Cream butter and sugar in a large bowl until fluffy.
2. Beat in egg yolks, flour, salt, milk, lemon peel, and lemon juice.

3. In a separate bowl, beat egg whites until stiff, then fold into the milk mixture.
4. Pour into an unbaked pie shell.
5. Bake at 375°F for 15 minutes, then reduce heat to 300°F and bake an additional 45 minutes until top is golden.

## Buttermilk Pie

*Recipe by Elizabeth Greene, Delaware, OH*

**Ingredients:**

- 3 eggs
- 2 cups sugar
- 1 Tbsp flour
- 2/3 cup buttermilk

- 1/2 cup melted butter
- 1 1/2 tsp vanilla
- Pinch of salt

**Instructions:**

1. Preheat oven to 300°F.
2. In a bowl, beat eggs with sugar until smooth, then add flour, buttermilk, melted butter, vanilla, and salt.
3. Pour mixture into an unbaked 9-inch pie shell and bake at 275°F for 10 minutes. Increase temperature to 300°F and bake for an additional 50 minutes or until filling is set.

## Southern Pecan Pie

*Recipe by Mildred Buford*

**Ingredients:**

- 3 eggs, beaten
- 2/3 cup sugar
- Dash of salt

- 1 cup dark corn syrup
- 1/3 cup melted butter
- 1 cup pecan halves

**Instructions:**

1. Preheat oven to 350°F.
2. In a bowl, beat eggs with sugar, salt, corn syrup, and melted butter.
3. Stir in pecan halves and pour mixture into a prepared pie crust.
4. Bake for 50 minutes or until the filling is firm around the edges and slightly less set in the center.

## Paper Bag Apple Pie

*Recipe by Betty Williams*

**Ingredients:**

- 3-4 large baking apples, peeled, cored, and quartered
- 1/2 cup sugar
- 2 Tbsp flour
- 1/2 tsp cinnamon or nutmeg
- 2 Tbsp lemon juice
- 1/2 cup sugar (for topping)
- 1/2 cup butter, softened
- 1/2 cup flour (for topping)
- 1 (9-inch) unbaked pie shell

**Instructions:**

1. Preheat oven to 425°F.
2. In a bowl, toss apples with sugar, flour, and cinnamon or nutmeg.
3. Spoon apple mixture into the pie shell, drizzle with lemon juice.
4. For the topping, mix sugar, butter, and flour until crumbly, then sprinkle over apples.
5. Place pie in a large brown paper bag, fold the open end twice, and secure with paper clips.
6. Place bagged pie on a baking sheet and bake for 1 hour. Remove from bag and cool before serving.

## Deluxe Pecan Pie

*Recipe by Elizabeth Greene, Delaware, OH*

**Ingredients:**

- 1 (9-inch) unbaked pie shell
- 3 eggs, slightly beaten
- 1 cup dark Karo corn syrup
- 1 cup sugar
- 2 Tbsp margarine, melted
- 1 tsp vanilla extract
- 1 cup pecans

**Instructions:**

1. Preheat oven to 400°F.
2. In a bowl, combine eggs, corn syrup, sugar, melted margarine, and vanilla.

3. Stir in pecans and pour mixture into the unbaked pie shell.
4. Bake at 400°F for 15 minutes, then reduce heat to 350°F and bake for 30-35 minutes.

## Norwegian Apple Pie

*Recipe by Beverly Rose*

**Ingredients:**

- 3 eggs, unbeaten
- 1/2 cup sugar
- 1 cup sifted flour
- 2 tsp baking powder
- 1/2 tsp salt
- 1 tsp vanilla extract
- 1 cup chopped nuts
- 2 cups diced apples

**Instructions:**

1. Preheat oven to 325°F.
2. In a mixing bowl, beat eggs and gradually add sugar. Stir in flour, baking powder, salt, and vanilla.
3. Fold in nuts and apples.
4. Pour batter into a greased 9-inch pie pan and bake for 30-35 minutes. Serve with whipped cream or ice cream.

## Impossible Pie

*Recipe by Lucille Place*

**Ingredients**

- 1/2 cup Bisquick
- 2 cups milk
- 4 eggs
- 1/4 cup margarine
- 1 tsp vanilla
- 1/2 tsp nutmeg
- 1/2 cup coconut
- 1 cup sugar

**Instructions**

1. Mix all ingredients in a blender or with a mixer until smooth.
2. Pour mixture into a 10-inch pie pan.
3. Bake at 350°F for 35 minutes or until set.

## Texas Millionaire Pie

*Recipe by Ona W. Goff*

### Ingredients:

- 2 cups powdered sugar
- 1 stick margarine, softened
- 1 large egg
- 1/4 tsp salt
- 1/4 tsp vanilla
- 2 (8-inch) baked pie shells
- 1 cup crushed pineapple, drained
- 1/2 cup chopped nuts
- 1 cup whipped cream or La Creme

### Instructions:

1. In a bowl, cream powdered sugar and margarine, then add egg, salt, and vanilla. Mix until light and fluffy.
2. Spoon mixture evenly into baked pie shells and chill.
3. Whip cream until stiff, then fold in pineapple and nuts. Spread whipped cream mixture over the egg filling in pie shells.
4. Chill thoroughly before serving. Makes two 8-inch pies.

## HANDY CAKE PAN CHART
### ROUND PANS

- **6×2-inch round pan:** Holds 4 cups of batter; equivalent to an 8×4-inch loaf pan. (Cupcake recipes yielding 12–16 cupcakes fit well in three 6-inch cake pans.)
- **8×2-inch round pan:** Holds 6 cups of batter.
- **9×2-inch round pan:** Holds 8 cups of batter; equivalent to an 8×2-inch square pan and a 9×5-inch loaf pan.
- **10×2-inch round pan:** Holds 10–11 cups of batter; equivalent to a 9×2 inch square pan, 11×7 inch pan, 10×3 inch Bundt pan, and a 9×2.5-inch springform pan.

### Square Pans

- **8×2-inch square pan:** Holds 8 cups of batter; equivalent to a 9×2 inch round pan and a 9×5 inch loaf pan.
- **9×2-inch square pan:** Holds 10 cups of batter; equivalent to a 10×2 inch round pan, 11×7 inch pan, 9×2.5-inch springform pan, and a 10×3 inch Bundt pan.
- **10×2-inch square pan:** Holds 12 cups of batter; equivalent to a 10×3 inch Bundt pan, 10×2.5-inch springform pan, and a 9-inch tube pan.

### Rectangle Pans

- **11×7 inch pan:** Holds 10 cups of batter; equivalent to a 10×2 inch round pan, 9×2-inch square pan, 9×2.5-inch springform pan, and 10×3 inch Bundt pan.
- **9×13 inch pan:** Holds 14–16 cups of batter; equivalent to two 9×2-inch round pans.

∾

## Loaf Cake

*Recipe by Ella Jones*

### Ingredients:

1 lb. butter
3 cups cake flour
5 eggs

2 tsp. vanilla
1 lb. confectioners' sugar

### Instructions:

1. Cream butter and sugar gradually.

2. Add eggs one at a time, mixing well.
3. Add vanilla.
4. Bake at 350°F for 40 minutes.

## Cheesecake

*Recipe by Paul Holliman*

**Ingredients:**

1/3 cup melted butter
3 Tbsp. sugar
1½ cups graham cracker crumbs
1 (8 oz.) pkg. cream cheese, softened

1 (14 oz.) can sweetened condensed milk
1/3 cup lemon juice (fresh or bottled)
1 tsp. vanilla
1 (21 oz.) can cherry pie filling

**Instructions:**

1. In a 9-inch pie pan, mix graham cracker crumbs, 3 Tbsp sugar, and melted butter. Press firmly over the bottom and sides of the pan. Bake at 350°F for 10–15 minutes.
2. In a medium bowl, beat softened cream cheese until light and fluffy. Gradually add sweetened condensed milk, beating until smooth. Stir in lemon juice and vanilla until well mixed.
3. Pour filling into the crust. Chill for 3 hours until firm, then top with cherry pie filling.

## Cherry Cheesecake Pie

**Ingredients:**

1 Keebler ready-made graham cracker pie crust
1 (8 oz.) pkg. cream cheese, softened
1/3 cup sugar

1 cup (1/2 pint) sour cream
2 tsp. vanilla
1 (8 oz.) container Cool Whip, thawed
1 cup cherry pie filling

**Instructions:**

1. Beat cream cheese until smooth; gradually beat in sugar. Blend in sour cream and vanilla. Fold in whipped topping, blending well.
2. Spoon mixture into the crust; chill until set, at least 4 hours. Top with cherry pie filling.

## Baked Cheesecake

**Ingredients:**

| | |
|---|---|
| 4 Tbsp. sugar | 1½ cups sugar |
| 26 graham crackers, crushed fine | 4 eggs, slightly beaten |
| 1 stick and 2 Tbsp. butter | 3 tsp. vanilla |
| 1½ lbs. cream cheese | |

**Instructions:**

1. Mix the first three ingredients and press into a lined 9-inch springform pan. Set in refrigerator to cool.
2. Cream sugar and cream cheese for 5–10 minutes. When well creamed, add eggs and vanilla. Beat the mixture on slow speed for 30 minutes.
3. Bake for 60 minutes at 300°F. Remove from oven and cool for 20 minutes.

**Topping:**

| | |
|---|---|
| ¾ pt. sour cream | 3 tsp. vanilla |
| 3–4 Tbsp. sugar | |

**Instructions for Topping:**

1. Mix and spread on top of the cooled cheesecake.
2. Return to oven for 10 minutes.

## Pudding Cheesecake

*Recipe by Janice Hudgens*

**Ingredients:**

| | |
|---|---|
| 1 box Jiffy yellow or white cake mix | 2 pkgs. vanilla instant pudding |
| 1 (20 oz.) can crushed pineapple, drained | 2 cups milk |
| 1 (8 oz.) pkg. cream cheese | 1 (8 oz.) container Cool Whip, thawed |
| ½ cup pineapple juice | Toasted coconut (optional) |
| | Pinch of salt |

**Instructions:**

1. Prepare the cake according to package directions, bake in a 9 x 13-inch pan, and cool completely.
2. Spread crushed pineapple evenly over the cooled cake.

3. In a bowl, beat cream cheese, pineapple juice, and salt until fluffy. Add pudding mix and milk, blending well.
4. Fold in Cool Whip, then spread over the pineapple. Sprinkle with toasted coconut if desired.

# Chocolate Chip Streusel Cake

*Recipe by Lois Heath*

### Ingredients:

¾ cup flour
¾ cup packed brown sugar
2 tsp. cinnamon
¼ cup butter or margarine, softened
1 (6 oz.) pkg. semi-sweet chocolate chips

1 pkg. Betty Crocker yellow cake mix
4 eggs
1 cup water
½ cup butter or margarine, softened

### Instructions:

1. Preheat oven to 350°F and grease a 12-cup Bundt pan.
2. Mix flour, brown sugar, cinnamon, and ¼ cup butter until crumbly, then stir in chocolate chips.
3. In a large bowl, blend cake mix, eggs, water, and ½ cup butter on low speed until moistened. Beat on medium speed for 3 minutes.
4. Pour half the batter into the pan, sprinkle with crumb mixture, then add remaining batter.
5. Bake for 40–45 minutes or until a toothpick comes out clean. Cool in the pan for 20 minutes, then invert onto a wire rack to cool completely. Dust with powdered sugar if desired.

# German Chocolate Cake

*Recipe by Donna Flournoy*

### Ingredients:

1 (4 oz.) pkg. Baker's German's Sweet Chocolate
½ cup boiling water
1 cup butter or margarine
2 cups sugar
4 egg yolks

1 tsp. vanilla
2¼ cups sifted all-purpose flour
1 tsp. baking soda
½ tsp. salt
1 cup buttermilk
4 egg whites, stiffly beaten

# Delicious Ideas!

## Instructions:

1. Preheat oven to 350°F. Line three 9-inch cake pans with parchment on the bottom.
2. Melt chocolate in boiling water; cool.
3. Cream butter and sugar until light and fluffy. Add egg yolks one at a time, beating well after each. Blend in vanilla and chocolate.
4. Sift flour with baking soda and salt. Add alternately with buttermilk, beating well after each addition.
5. Fold in beaten egg whites. Pour into prepared pans.
6. Bake for 30–35 minutes or until the cake springs back when lightly pressed in the center. Cool in pans for 15 minutes, then remove and cool on racks.

## Coconut Pecan Filling and Frosting:

| | |
|---|---|
| 1 cup evaporated milk | 1 tsp. vanilla |
| 1 cup sugar | 1½ cups Baker's Angel Flake |
| 3 egg yolks | coconut |
| ½ cup butter or margarine | 1 cup chopped pecans |

## Instructions for Frosting:

1. Combine milk, sugar, egg yolks, butter, and vanilla in a saucepan. Cook over medium heat, stirring constantly until thickened, about 12 minutes.
2. Remove from heat, then stir in coconut and pecans. Cool until of spreading consistency before applying between cake layers and on top.

# Oatmeal Cake

*Recipe by Naomi Bauer*

## Ingredients:

| | |
|---|---|
| 1¼ cup boiling water | 1 tsp. cinnamon |
| 1 cup quick-cooking oats | ¼ tsp. nutmeg |
| ½ cup shortening | ½ tsp. salt |
| 1 cup brown sugar | 1⅓ cup flour |
| 1 cup white sugar | 1 tsp. baking soda |
| 2 eggs | |

## Instructions:

1. Preheat oven to 350°F. Grease and flour a 9-inch square pan.
2. Pour boiling water over oats and let sit for 20 minutes.
3. Mix in shortening, both sugars, eggs, cinnamon, nutmeg, and salt until well combined.

4. Sift flour and baking soda, then add to oat mixture, blending well.
5. Pour batter into prepared pan and bake for 35–40 minutes.

**Broiler Topping:**

| | |
|---|---|
| 6 Tbsp. melted butter | 1 cup coconut |
| ½ cup hot canned milk | ½ cup chopped nuts |
| ½ cup brown sugar | 1 tsp. vanilla |

**Instructions for Topping:**

1. Mix all ingredients for topping. Spread on the hot cake.
2. Place under broiler until bubbly.

## Texas Chocolate Sheet Cake

*Recipe by Ruth Faulkner*

**Ingredients:**

| | |
|---|---|
| 2 cups flour | ½ cup buttermilk |
| 2 cups sugar | 2 eggs |
| 1 stick oleo (margarine) | 1 tsp. baking soda |
| ½ cup shortening | ½ tsp. salt |
| 3 Tbsp. cocoa | 1 tsp. vanilla |
| 1 cup water | |

**Instructions:**

1. Preheat oven to 400°F. Grease an 11 x 16-inch pan.
2. In a mixing bowl, combine flour and sugar.
3. In a saucepan, combine oleo, shortening, cocoa, and water, bringing to a boil. Pour over flour and sugar mixture.
4. Mix well, then add buttermilk, eggs, baking soda, salt, and vanilla. Blend until smooth.
5. Bake for 20 minutes.

**Icing for Texas Sheet Cake:**

| | |
|---|---|
| 1 stick oleo (margarine) | 1 tsp. vanilla |
| 3 Tbsp. cocoa | 1 box powdered sugar |
| 6 Tbsp. milk | 1 cup chopped pecans |

**Instructions for Icing:**

1. Start icing when cake comes out of the oven. In a saucepan, bring oleo, cocoa, milk, and vanilla to a boil.

Delicious Ideas!

2. Stir in powdered sugar and pecans. Mix well and pour over the warm cake.

## Christmas Cakes

*Recipe by Donna Downing*

**Ingredients:**

| | |
|---|---|
| 3 cups sugar | 8–9 cups flour |
| 3 tsp. baking powder | 1 cup sour cream |
| 3 eggs | 2 cups buttermilk |
| 1 level cup lard | 2 tsp. baking soda (dissolved in a |
| 1 tsp. salt | little hot water) |

**Instructions:**

1. In a large bowl, mix dry ingredients alternately with the liquid ingredients until well blended.
2. Chill dough before rolling out.
3. Preheat oven to 375°F to 450°F, depending on the oven.
4. Roll out dough and cut into desired shapes.
5. Bake for 12–15 minutes until lightly golden.

## Jam Cake

*Recipe by Miss John Ellen Steele*

**Ingredients:**

| | |
|---|---|
| 4 eggs | 1 cup buttermilk with 1 tsp. |
| 1 cup white sugar | baking soda stirred in |
| 1 cup brown sugar | 1 cup jam |
| 1 cup butter or margarine | 1 tsp. cinnamon |
| 4 cups flour | 1 tsp. cloves |
| 1 cup molasses | 1 Tbsp. chocolate syrup or cocoa |
| | 1 cup chopped raisins or nuts |

**Instructions:**

1. In a large mixing bowl, beat eggs, sugar, spices, butter, molasses, and buttermilk together until smooth.
2. Gradually add flour, mixing well after each addition.
3. Mix on high speed for 3 minutes, then fold in jam, raisins, and nuts.
4. Pour batter into a greased angel food cake pan.
5. Bake at 350°F for 1 hour and 15 minutes or until a toothpick inserted comes out clean.

**Cream Cheese Frosting:**

½ cup margarine (1 stick)
1 (8 oz.) pkg. cream cheese, softened

1 lb. box confectioners' sugar
1 tsp. vanilla

**Instructions for Frosting:**

1. In a mixing bowl, cream margarine, cream cheese, and vanilla.
2. Gradually add confectioners' sugar, beating until smooth.
3. Spread frosting over the cooled cake.

# Pineapple Upside-Down Cake

*Recipe by Mary Morall*

**Ingredients for Cake:**

1½ cups flour
1 cup sugar
1 tsp. baking powder
½ cup melted butter

½ cup milk
1 egg
1 tsp. vanilla

**Ingredients for Sauce:**

1 cup brown sugar
4 Tbsp. buttermilk

1 can sliced pineapple (without syrup)

**Instructions:**

1. Preheat oven to 350°F. Grease a baking dish.
2. For the cake, mix flour, sugar, and baking powder in a bowl. Separately, combine melted butter, milk, egg, and vanilla. Pour the wet mixture into the dry ingredients and mix until smooth.
3. For the sauce, cook brown sugar and buttermilk in a small pan until thickened.
4. Pour sauce over the pineapple slices arranged in the greased baking dish.
5. Pour cake batter over the sauce and bake for 35–40 minutes until golden and set.

## Red Velvet Cake

*Recipe by Loria Bohanna Moore*

### Ingredients for Cake:

| | |
|---|---|
| 3 cups flour | 1 tsp. baking soda |
| 2½ cups sugar | ¼ tsp. salt |
| 4 eggs | 1 Tbsp. vinegar |
| 3 Tbsp. cocoa | 1 tsp. vanilla |
| 2 cups Wesson oil | ½ oz. red food coloring |
| 1 cup buttermilk | |

### Instructions:

1. Preheat oven to 350°F. Grease three 9-inch round cake pans.
2. In a large mixing bowl, combine all cake ingredients.
3. Beat on medium speed until smooth and the color is even.
4. Divide batter among prepared pans and bake for 25–30 minutes or until a toothpick inserted comes out clean.
5. Cool layers completely before frosting.

### Cream Cheese Frosting:

| | |
|---|---|
| 1 stick butter | 1 box powdered sugar |
| 1 (8 oz.) pkg. cream cheese | 1 tsp. vanilla |

### Instructions for Frosting:

1. Cream all ingredients until smooth and fluffy.
2. Frost each layer, then the top and sides of the cake.

## Carrot Cake

### Ingredients

| | |
|---|---|
| 3 cups carrots, chopped | 1 tsp baking soda |
| 2 cups sugar | 2 tsp cinnamon |
| 2 1/4 cups flour | 1 tsp salt |
| 4 eggs | 1 cup chopped nuts (English walnuts) |
| 1 1/2 cup oil | |

### Instructions

1. In a large bowl, beat carrots and oil together until well mixed.
2. Add eggs one at a time, beating after each addition.
3. Gradually blend in dry ingredients until well incorporated.

4.  Lightly flour and grease a baking pan.
5.  Pour batter into prepared pan and bake at 325°F for 30 to 35 minutes, or until a toothpick inserted in the center comes out clean.

# Carrot Cake

*Recipe by Mildred Buford*

### Ingredients

1 1/2 cups vegetable oil
2 cups sugar
4 eggs
2 cups flour
2 tsp cinnamon

2 tsp baking soda
2 tsp baking powder
1/2 tsp salt
2 cans carrots, mashed
1 cup nuts

### Instructions

1.  In a large bowl, mix oil and sugar until well combined.
2.  Add eggs one at a time, blending well after each addition.
3.  Mix in dry ingredients, then gently fold in the mashed carrots and nuts.
4.  Pour batter into a greased baking pan.
5.  Bake at 350°F for 30 to 35 minutes or until a toothpick inserted in the center comes out clean.

# Carrot Cake

*Recipe by Kimberly Strain*

### Ingredients:

3 cups carrots, chopped
2 cups sugar
2¼ cups flour
4 eggs
1½ cups oil

1 tsp. baking soda
2 tsp. cinnamon
1 tsp. salt
1 cup chopped nuts (English walnuts preferred)

### Instructions:

1.  Preheat oven to 325°F. Grease and flour a 9x13-inch pan.
2.  In a large bowl, beat carrots and oil, then add eggs one at a time, mixing well after each.
3.  Add sugar, flour, baking soda, cinnamon, and salt, blending well.
4.  Stir in chopped nuts.
5.  Pour batter into the prepared pan and bake for 30–35 minutes or until a toothpick comes out clean.

Delicious Ideas!

### Cream Cheese Frosting:

½ cup margarine (1 stick)
1 (8 oz.) pkg. cream cheese, softened

1 lb. box confectioners' sugar
1 tsp. vanilla

### Instructions for Frosting:

1. Cream margarine, cream cheese, and vanilla, then add sugar and beat until smooth.
2. Spread frosting over the cooled cake.

## Banana Cake

*Recipe by Marietta Bell*

### Ingredients

1 1/3 cup sugar
1/2 cup shortening
2 eggs, beaten together
4 Tbsp sour milk
1 tsp vanilla
2 cups flour

1 tsp baking powder
1 tsp baking soda
1/2 tsp salt
1/2 cup raisins
1 cup mashed bananas

### Instructions

1. Preheat oven to 350°F.
2. In a large bowl, mix all ingredients together until well combined.
3. Grease a baking pan well and lightly flour the bottom.
4. Pour batter into the prepared pan.
5. Bake for 35 to 40 minutes, or until a toothpick inserted in the center comes out clean.

### Scripture Cake

*Recipe by Sis Ona W. Goff*

### Ingredients

1 cup butter (Judges 5:25)
2 cups sugar (Jeremiah 6:20)
6 eggs (Isaiah 10:14)
3 1/2 cups flour (I Kings 4:22)
3 1/2 tsp baking powder (Amos 4:5)
1/2 tsp salt (Leviticus 2:13)
1/2 tsp cinnamon (I Kings 10:2)
1/4 tsp cloves (I Kings 10:2)

1/4 tsp ginger (I Kings 10:2)
1/2 tsp nutmeg (I Kings 10:2)
1/4 tsp allspice (I Kings 10:2)
1 cup water (Genesis 26:20)
2 cups diced figs or dates (I Samuel 30:12)
2 cups raisins (I Samuel 30:12)
1 cup nuts (Genesis 43:11)

**Instructions**

1. Preheat oven to 325°F. Grease and flour a 10-inch tube pan.
2. Cream butter and sugar in a large bowl.
3. Add eggs one at a time, beating well after each addition.
4. Sift together flour, baking powder, salt, and spices.
5. Add sifted dry ingredients to creamed mixture alternately with water.
6. Dredge fruits and nuts in a small amount of flour, then fold into the batter.
7. Pour batter into the prepared pan.
8. Bake for approximately 2 hours or until done.

# Coconut Apple Nut Cake

*Recipe by Shirley Chaffin*

**Ingredients:**

| | |
|---|---|
| 2 cups sugar | 1 tsp. salt |
| 1½ cups vegetable oil | 1 tsp. vanilla |
| 3 eggs | 3 cups peeled, diced apples |
| 1 tsp. soda | 1 cup coconut |
| 3 cups flour | 1 cup chopped nuts |

**Instructions:**

1. Preheat oven to 350°F. In a large bowl, combine sugar, oil, eggs, vanilla, apples, coconut, and nuts.
2. Separately, mix flour, soda, and salt, then stir into the wet mixture until combined.
3. Pour into an ungreased tube pan.
4. Bake for 1 hour and 20 minutes, or until a toothpick inserted in the center comes out clean.

**Icing:**

| | |
|---|---|
| 1 lb. powdered sugar | 1 tsp. vanilla |
| ½ cup butter | |

**Instructions for Icing:**

1. In a mixing bowl, cream powdered sugar with butter and vanilla until smooth.
2. Spread over cooled cake.

## American Liberian Pound Cake

*Recipe by Loria Bohanna Moore*

**Ingredients:**

| | |
|---|---|
| 1 lb. butter | 4 tsp. baking powder |
| 2 cups sugar | 2½ cups flour |
| 4 eggs | 1 tsp. vanilla |
| 1 cup evaporated milk | |

**Instructions:**

1. Preheat oven to 350°F.
2. Cream butter and sugar together until light and fluffy.
3. Add eggs one at a time, beating after each addition. Stir in vanilla and evaporated milk.
4. Sift flour with baking powder, then add to the butter mixture gradually, mixing until smooth.
5. Pour batter into a greased and floured cake pan and bake until a toothpick inserted in the center comes out clean.

## Pound Cake

*Recipe by Kimberly Strain*

**Ingredients:**

| | |
|---|---|
| 1 cup butter | 2 cups all-purpose flour, sifted 3 times |
| 2 cups sugar | |
| 6 large eggs | 1 tsp. vanilla |

**Instructions:**

1. Preheat oven to 290°F. Grease and line a tube pan with parchment paper.
2. Cream butter in a mixer until smooth. Gradually add sugar, beating well.
3. Add eggs one at a time, mixing thoroughly after each addition.
4. Add vanilla, then gradually incorporate the sifted flour, mixing until well blended.
5. Pour batter into the prepared pan. Bake at 290°F for 40 minutes, then increase oven temperature to 325°F and bake an additional 40 minutes. Do not open the oven door during baking.
6. Let cool in the pan for 10 minutes before turning out onto a wire rack to cool completely.

# Seven-Up Cake

*Recipe by Kimberly Strain*

**Ingredients:**

| | |
|---|---|
| 3 cups flour | 5 eggs |
| 3 sticks butter, softened | ¾ cup Seven-Up |
| 3 cups sugar | 1 Tbsp. lemon extract |

**Instructions:**

1. Preheat oven to 350°F. Grease and flour a Bundt or tube pan.
2. In a large mixing bowl, cream butter and sugar until light and fluffy.
3. Add eggs one at a time, beating well after each addition.
4. Gradually add flour, mixing until smooth, then stir in Seven-Up and lemon extract.
5. Pour batter into the prepared pan and bake for about 1 hour or until a toothpick inserted into the center comes out clean.
6. Let cake cool in the pan for 15 minutes, then turn out onto a rack to cool completely.

# Flannel Cakes

*Recipe by Ella Jones*

**Ingredients:**

| | |
|---|---|
| 2 cups flour | 3 eggs, separated |
| 2 tsp. baking powder | 2 cups milk |
| ½ tsp. salt | ½ cup butter, melted |

**Instructions:**

1. In a large bowl, sift together flour, baking powder, and salt.
2. Beat egg yolks and add to the dry ingredients along with milk and melted butter, mixing until smooth.
3. In a separate bowl, beat egg whites until stiff peaks form, then gently fold into the batter.
4. Pour batter by spoonfuls onto a hot, lightly greased griddle. Cook until bubbles appear on the surface and the edges are golden, then flip and cook until the other side is golden.
5. Serve warm with butter and syrup. Makes about 30 pancakes.

## Chocolate Cake

*Recipe by Bev Rose*

### Ingredients:

¾ cup butter or margarine, softened
1¾ cups sugar
2 eggs
1 tsp. vanilla

2 cups all-purpose flour
¾ cup Hershey's cocoa
1¼ tsp. baking soda
½ tsp. salt
1⅓ cups water

### Instructions:

1. Preheat oven to 350°F. Grease and flour two 8-inch round cake pans.
2. In a large bowl, cream together butter and sugar until light and fluffy. Add eggs and vanilla, beating until smooth.
3. In another bowl, sift together flour, cocoa, baking soda, and salt.
4. Add the dry ingredients alternately with water to the creamed mixture, mixing until smooth.
5. Divide batter evenly between prepared pans and bake for 35–40 minutes, or until a toothpick inserted in the center comes out clean.
6. Cool in pans for 10 minutes, then turn out onto wire racks to cool completely. Frost with your favorite chocolate frosting.

## Strawberry Cake

*Recipe by Barbara Jordan*

### Ingredients:

1 box white cake mix
1 small box strawberry Jell-O (optional)
3 Tbsp. flour
1 cup oil

½ cup milk
4 eggs, beaten
1 box frozen strawberries, thawed

### Topping:

1 box frozen strawberries, thawed

1 stick butter
1 cup powdered sugar

### Instructions:

1. Preheat oven to 375°F. Grease and flour a 9x13-inch cake pan.
2. In a large mixing bowl, combine cake mix, Jell-O (if using), flour, oil, milk, and eggs. Mix until smooth, then fold in thawed strawberries.

3. Pour batter into prepared pan and bake for 45 minutes or until a toothpick inserted in the center comes out clean.
4. For the topping, melt butter in a saucepan, add strawberries and powdered sugar, and heat until well combined.
5. Poke holes in the baked cake with a fork and pour the topping over it, allowing it to absorb.

# Mandarin Orange Cake

*Recipe by Alice Salisbury*

### Ingredients for Cake:

1 box yellow cake mix
4 eggs
1 cup oil

1 small can mandarin oranges with juice

### Icing:

1 (8 oz.) container Cool Whip
1 small pkg. instant vanilla pudding, dry

1 large can crushed pineapple with juice

### Instructions:

1. Preheat oven to 350°F. Grease and flour a 9x13-inch pan.
2. In a mixing bowl, beat cake mix, eggs, oil, and mandarin oranges with juice for 2 minutes.
3. Pour into prepared pan and bake for 30–35 minutes or until a toothpick inserted in the center comes out clean.
4. For the icing, mix Cool Whip, dry pudding mix, and crushed pineapple with juice. Spread over the cooled cake and refrigerate until ready to serve.

# Cherry Cake

*Recipe by Juanita Schultz*

### Ingredients

1 box cherry cake mix
2/3 box cherry Jello
2/3 stick margarine, melted

1 1/3 cup water
2 egg whites

### Instructions

1. Preheat oven to 350°F.
2. In a large mixing bowl, combine cake mix and jello.
3. Add melted butter and water, stirring until mixture is moist.

# Delicious Ideas!

4. Beat egg whites until foamy and add to mixture, stirring thoroughly.
5. Pour batter into a greased baking pan.
6. Bake for about 25 minutes or until a toothpick inserted in the center comes out clean.

## Summer Cake

Recipe by Icie Mayes

**Ingredients:**

1 pkg. yellow cake mix
4 eggs

1 can mandarin oranges with juice
3 Tbsp. Crisco oil

**Icing:**

1 bowl Cool Whip
1 pkg. vanilla instant pudding

1 can crushed pineapple

**Instructions:**

1. Preheat oven to 425°F. Grease and flour three 8-inch cake pans.
2. In a large mixing bowl, beat cake mix, eggs, mandarin oranges, and oil with a mixer for 2 minutes until smooth and well-blended.
3. Divide batter evenly among the prepared pans and bake for 1 hour or until a toothpick inserted into the center comes out clean.
4. For the icing, combine Cool Whip, pudding, and crushed pineapple. Spread over each layer and top of the cooled cakes. Refrigerate until ready to serve.

## Peanut Butter Cookies

*Recipe by Cheri Morall*

**Ingredients:**

1½ cups shortening
1 cup brown sugar
1 cup granulated sugar
2 eggs
1 cup peanut butter

2 tsp. vanilla
4 cups all-purpose flour
1 tsp. salt
1 tsp. baking soda
1 tsp. baking powder

**Instructions:**

1. Preheat oven to 375°F.

2. In a large mixing bowl, cream together shortening and both sugars until light and fluffy.
3. Beat in eggs, peanut butter, and vanilla until well combined.
4. In another bowl, sift together flour, salt, baking soda, and baking powder. Gradually add dry ingredients to the creamed mixture, mixing until smooth.
5. Roll dough into small balls and place on a greased cookie sheet. Press down with a fork in a crisscross pattern.
6. Bake for 10–12 minutes, or until lightly golden. Transfer to a wire rack to cool completely.

## Sugar Cookies

*Recipe by Patti Banks*

**Ingredients:**

| | |
|---|---|
| 1 cup shortening | 1½ tsp. baking powder |
| ½ cup sugar | ¾ tsp. salt |
| 1 egg | Milk and additional sugar (for |
| 1 tsp. lemon extract | topping) |
| 2¼ cups flour | |

**Instructions:**

1. Preheat oven to 400°F.
2. Cream together shortening and ½ cup sugar until smooth. Beat in egg and lemon extract until well mixed.
3. In another bowl, sift together flour, baking powder, and salt. Add to the creamed mixture, mixing until smooth.
4. Shape dough into rolls about 2 inches in diameter. Wrap in wax paper and chill until firm.
5. Slice dough ⅛-inch thick, place on a greased baking sheet, brush with milk, and sprinkle with sugar.
6. Bake for 6 minutes, or until edges are lightly golden. Cool on a wire rack.

## Chocolate Chip Cookies

*Recipe by Barbara Jordan*

**Ingredients:**

| | |
|---|---|
| 2¼ cups sifted flour | 1 tsp. vanilla |
| 1 tsp. baking soda | ½ tsp. water |
| 1 tsp. salt | 2 eggs |
| 1 cup softened butter | 1 large package or 2 cups |
| ¾ cup granulated sugar | chocolate chips |
| ¾ cup firmly packed brown sugar | 1 cup chopped nuts (optional) |

Delicious Ideas!

**Instructions:**

1. Preheat oven to 375°F.
2. In a large mixing bowl, cream together butter, both sugars, vanilla, and water until creamy. Beat in the eggs one at a time.
3. In another bowl, sift together flour, baking soda, and salt. Gradually add to the creamed mixture, stirring until well combined.
4. Fold in chocolate chips and nuts (if using).
5. Drop by rounded teaspoonfuls onto a greased cookie sheet.
6. Bake for 10–12 minutes, or until edges are golden. Let cool on a wire rack. Makes approximately 100 cookies.

## Chocolate Crinkles

*Recipe by Joan Morall*

**Ingredients:**

| | |
|---|---|
| 1½ cups granulated sugar | 3 eggs |
| ½ cup cooking oil | ¼ cup milk |
| 3 (1 oz.) squares unsweetened chocolate, melted and cooled | 2 cups all-purpose flour |
| 2 tsp. vanilla | 2 tsp. baking powder |
| | Powdered sugar, for rolling |

**Instructions:**

1. Preheat oven to 375°F.
2. In a large mixing bowl, combine sugar, oil, melted chocolate, and vanilla. Add eggs one at a time, beating well after each addition. Stir in milk.
3. In a separate bowl, sift together flour and baking powder. Gradually add to the chocolate mixture, stirring until smooth.
4. Chill dough for 1 hour.
5. Using a tablespoon of dough for each cookie, shape into balls, then roll in powdered sugar.
6. Place on greased cookie sheets and bake for 10–12 minutes. While cookies are still warm, roll in powdered sugar again if desired. Makes approximately 4 dozen.

## Candy Cookies

*Recipe by Lois Health*

**Ingredients:**

| | |
|---|---|
| 2 cups sugar | 1 cup coconut |
| 1 stick oleo (butter substitute) | 1 cup chopped nuts |
| ½ cup milk | 1 cup butterscotch or chocolate bits |
| 3 cups oatmeal | |

**Instructions:**

1. In a saucepan, bring sugar, oleo, and milk to a boil.
2. Remove from heat and stir in oatmeal, coconut, nuts, and butterscotch or chocolate bits.
3. Drop by teaspoonfuls onto waxed paper and let cool until firm.

## Icebox Cookies

*Recipe by Sis Ona W. Goff*

**Ingredients:**

| | |
|---|---|
| ½ cup butter (no substitutes) | ½ tsp. baking powder |
| ¾ cup granulated sugar | ½ tsp. salt |
| 1 egg | 2 tsp. vanilla |
| 1¾ cups all-purpose flour, sifted | ½ cup chopped nuts |

**Instructions:**

1. Cream together butter and sugar until light and fluffy. Beat in the egg.
2. In a separate bowl, sift together flour, baking powder, and salt. Gradually add to the butter mixture, stirring until smooth.
3. Add vanilla and chopped nuts, mixing to combine.
4. Divide dough in half and roll each into a 6–7 inch log. Wrap in wax paper and refrigerate for 4 hours or overnight.
5. Preheat oven to 350°F. Slice dough ¼-inch thick and place on an ungreased cookie sheet. Bake for 10–12 minutes.

## Strawberry-Pineapple Crisp

*Recipe by Winifred Bondurant*

**Ingredients:**

| | |
|---|---|
| 1 (10 oz.) package frozen sliced strawberries, thawed | 2 Tbsp. flour |
| | 2 Tbsp. butter or margarine |
| 1 (20 oz.) can pineapple chunks in juice, drained | ⅛ tsp. ground cinnamon |
| | 2 Tbsp. brown sugar |
| ¾ cup quick cooking rolled oats | 2 Tbsp. cornstarch |
| ¼ cup brown sugar, packed | |

**Instructions:**

1. Preheat oven to 350°F. Grease a 10x6x2 inch baking dish.
2. Drain strawberries and pineapple, reserving juice. Add enough pineapple juice to the strawberry liquid to make 1 cup.

3. In a small saucepan, combine 2 tablespoons brown sugar and cornstarch. Gradually blend in the juice mixture and cook over medium heat, stirring constantly, until thickened, about 5 minutes. Pour over strawberries and pineapple in the prepared dish.
4. In a separate bowl, combine oats, ¼ cup brown sugar, and flour. Cut in butter until crumbly. Sprinkle over fruit mixture and add a dash of cinnamon.
5. Bake for 25–30 minutes, or until bubbly and golden around the edges.

# Cherry Delight

*Recipe by Eva Jordan*

**Ingredients:**

20 graham crackers, crushed
¼ cup sugar
½ cup melted butter
1 cup powdered sugar

1 large package Philadelphia cream cheese, softened
1 package Dream Whip, prepared according to package directions
2 cans cherry pie filling

**Instructions:**

1. In a 13x9-inch baking dish, combine crushed graham crackers, sugar, and melted butter. Press firmly into the bottom and refrigerate.
2. In a bowl, beat cream cheese and powdered sugar until very smooth.
3. Prepare Dream Whip as directed on the package, then fold into the cream cheese mixture. Spread over the graham cracker crust and refrigerate for 10 minutes.
4. Spread cherry pie filling evenly on top. Keep refrigerated until ready to serve.

# Raspberry Dessert

*Recipe by Lois Health*

**Ingredients:**

1 package raspberry gelatin
1½ cups boiling water

2 packages frozen raspberries, thawed and mashed
1-pint vanilla ice cream

**Instructions:**

1. Dissolve gelatin in boiling water in a large bowl. Add mashed raspberries and stir well.
2. Mix in the ice cream until it melts completely and blends with the gelatin.
3. Pour mixture into a serving dish and refrigerate until firm.

4. Optional: Top with whipped cream before serving.

## Summer Treat with Orange

*Recipe by Damita El Bannani*

**Ingredients:**

1 large box orange gelatin
1 large can crushed pineapple, undrained
1 small can mandarin oranges, undrained

1 large box lemon-flavored instant pudding
Cool Whip, for topping
Walnut halves, for garnish

**Instructions:**

1. Prepare orange gelatin with mandarin oranges and crushed pineapple in a large 13x9-inch baking dish. Chill until set.
2. Meanwhile, prepare lemon pudding according to package directions, allowing it to cool to room temperature.
3. Once gelatin has set, layer the lemon pudding over it. Spread a layer of Cool Whip on top of the pudding and garnish with walnut halves. Refrigerate until ready to serve.

## Chocolate-Mint Dessert

*Recipe by Lillie R. Kimbro*

**Ingredients:**

1 (5.5 oz.) can chocolate syrup
2 Tbsp. green crème de menthe
Brownies, for serving

Vanilla or chocolate-mint ice cream

**Instructions:**

1. In a small bowl, combine chocolate syrup and crème de menthe, stirring well.
2. Warm the sauce over low heat or serve cold, depending on preference.
3. Serve over brownies with a scoop of vanilla or chocolate-mint ice cream.

## Eagle Brand Pie

*Recipe by Terri Bohanna*

### Ingredients:

1 can condensed Eagle Brand milk
1 small can lemonade concentrate, thawed

1 large bowl Cool Whip, thawed
1 graham cracker pie crust

### Instructions:

1. In a mixing bowl, blend together condensed milk and lemonade concentrate until well combined.
2. Fold in Cool Whip until the mixture is fluffy.
3. Pour mixture into the graham cracker crust and freeze for at least 2 hours.
4. Slice and serve directly from the freezer.

## Umph

*Recipe by Ella Jones*

### Ingredients:

2 packages Philadelphia cream cheese, softened
1 large container whipped cream

1 medium-sized angel food cake, torn into bite-size pieces
1 large can cherry pie filling
1 small can cherry pie filling

### Instructions:

1. In a large mixing bowl, mash softened cream cheese with a fork until smooth.
2. Fold in whipped cream until well blended.
3. Gently mix in angel food cake pieces a little at a time, allowing the mixture to stay lumpy.
4. Spread mixture evenly in a large oblong cake pan. Spread both cans of cherry pie filling on top and refrigerate until serving.

# Pineapple Fluff Dessert

*Recipe by Jean Johnson*

## Ingredients:

1 egg
1 cup crushed pineapple, drained
1 cup sugar
1 small box lemon gelatin (dry)
Dash of salt

1 large can Pet milk, chilled
1 Tbsp. vanilla
1½ cups graham cracker crumbs
½ stick butter, melted

## Instructions:

1. In a saucepan, combine egg, pineapple, sugar, dry lemon gelatin, and salt. Bring to a boil over medium heat and cook until mixture thickens. Chill in the refrigerator until cool.
2. In a separate bowl, whip chilled Pet milk with 1 tablespoon of sugar and vanilla until light and fluffy. Fold in the chilled pineapple mixture.
3. In a casserole dish lined with graham cracker crumbs, pour the mixture and top with additional graham cracker crumbs. Chill until set.

# Cherry Dessert

*Recipe by Margaret Ann Law*

## Ingredients:

3 egg whites
1 cup sugar
1 cup soda cracker crumbs
1 cup chopped nuts

1 package whipped topping
(Lucky Whip or similar)
1 can cherry pie filling

## Instructions:

1. Preheat oven to 300°F.
2. In a bowl, beat egg whites until soft peaks form. Gradually add sugar, then fold in soda cracker crumbs and nuts.
3. Spread mixture evenly in a buttered 8x10-inch pan and bake for 30 minutes. Cool completely.
4. Spread whipped topping over the cooled crust, then spoon cherry pie filling on top.
5. Chill for at least 24 hours before serving.

## Mandarin Orange Dessert

*Recipe by Margaret Ann Law*

**Ingredients:**

1 cup white sugar
1 cup flour
1 tsp. baking soda
½ tsp. salt

1 (11 oz.) can mandarin oranges
with juice
½ cup brown sugar
½ cup chopped nutmeats

**Instructions:**

1. Preheat oven to 375°F. Grease an 8x8-inch baking dish.
2. In a bowl, beat together white sugar, flour, baking soda, salt, and the mandarin oranges with juice. Pour batter into the prepared dish.
3. In a small bowl, combine brown sugar and chopped nutmeats. Sprinkle this mixture over the batter.
4. Bake for 45 minutes or until golden brown.

## TROUBLESHOOTING ADVICE FOR JELLY MAKING

HERE'S a guide for troubleshooting common jelly-making problems:

- **Why Does It Get Cloudy?**
  - Possible causes:
    - Pouring the mixture into jars too slowly.
    - Allowing the mixture to sit before pouring.
    - Juice not properly strained, leaving pulp.
    - Using too-green fruit, causing rapid setting.
- **Why Do Crystals Form?**
  - Causes:
    - Too much sugar in the mixture.
    - Cooking too little, too slowly, or for too long.
    - Evaporation when an opened jar stands, causing crystals at the top.
    - In grape jellies, natural tartrate crystals may form.
- **Why Is It Syrupy?**
  - Causes:
    - Too little pectin, acid, or sugar.
    - Excess sugar can also result in a syrupy texture.
- **Why Is It Tough?**
  - Cause:
    - Cooking too long to reach the jellying stage, usually due to insufficient sugar.
- **Why Does Mold Form?**
  - Cause:
    - An imperfect seal allows mold and air into the jar.
- **What Causes It to Be Too Soft?**
  - Causes:
    - Too much juice in the mixture.
    - Too little sugar.
    - Insufficient acidity.
    - Making too large a batch at one time.

### TIPS FOR MAKING JELLY

- Use a vegetable brush to remove scum from the surface.
- If your jelly becomes sugary, use it as a syrup by adding half a glass of water to one glass of jelly and heating until dissolved.
- For hard or sugary jelly, leave it in a warm oven to soften.
- Avoid squeezing the juice bag when extracting juice for the clearest jelly.
- Too much sugar is often the primary cause of failure.
- Use equal parts of ripe and slightly under-ripe fruit for the best flavor.
- If jam fruit floats, let the jam set for an hour, turn the jar upside down, then return it to its upright position to distribute the fruit evenly.

## Cocoa Fudge Candy

*Recipe by Eva Jordan*

**Ingredients:**

⅔ cup cocoa
1½ cups evaporated milk
3 cups sugar

1 stick butter
Pinch of salt
1 tsp vanilla

**Instructions:**

1. Mix cocoa, sugar, and salt in a heavy 3-quart saucepan. Gradually add milk, mixing until smooth.
2. Bring mixture to a boil on high heat, stirring continuously. Reduce heat to medium and cook without stirring until it reaches the soft ball stage (about 1 hour).
3. Remove from heat and add butter and vanilla without stirring. Set the pan in cold water for about 20 minutes.
4. Beat until thick and glossy, about 10 minutes. Pour into a greased 8×8×2-inch pan. Makes approximately 3 dozen squares.

## Mamie Eisenhower's Fudge

**Ingredients:**

4½ cups sugar
2 Tbsp butter
Pinch of salt
1⅔ cups evaporated milk (1 tall can)

12 oz. semi-sweet chocolate bits
12 oz. German's sweet chocolate
1 pint marshmallow cream (2 jars)
2 cups nutmeats

**Instructions:**

1. In a saucepan, boil sugar, salt, butter, and evaporated milk for 6 minutes.
2. In a large bowl, combine chocolate bits, German's sweet chocolate, marshmallow cream, and nuts.
3. Pour the hot syrup over the mixture and beat until chocolate melts.
4. Pour into a pan and let set for several hours before cutting. Store in a tin box.

## Caramel Fudge

*Recipe by Lois Heath*

**Ingredients:**

1½ cups brown sugar
½ cup milk
3 cups sifted powdered sugar

¼ tsp salt
1 tsp vanilla

**Instructions:**

1. In a saucepan, combine brown sugar, salt, and milk. Bring to a boil and cook slowly for 5 minutes until slightly thickened.
2. Remove from heat, add margarine and vanilla, and cool. Add powdered sugar and beat until smooth.
3. Press into a greased pan and cool before cutting.

## Caramel Jumbles

*Recipe by Naomi Bauer*

**Ingredients:**

½ cup soft shortening
1 cup brown sugar, packed
½ cup granulated sugar
2 eggs
1 cup undiluted evaporated milk
1 tsp vanilla

2¾ cups sifted all-purpose flour
½ tsp baking soda
1 tsp salt
1 (8 oz.) package chocolate, butterscotch, or peanut butter bits
½ cup chopped nuts

**Instructions:**

1. Cream shortening, sugars, and eggs. Add evaporated milk and vanilla, then combine with sifted flour, baking soda, and salt.
2. Add bits and nuts and chill for 1 hour.
3. Drop by spoonfuls onto a baking sheet and bake at 375°F for 10 minutes. Frost with sour cream frosting if desired.

## Peanut Butter Bonbons

**Ingredients:**

1 can vanilla frosting
1 cup peanut butter
½ cup softened margarine

2 cups graham cracker crumbs
1 can any flavored frosting

**Instructions:**

1. In a bowl, combine vanilla frosting, peanut butter, and margarine. Add graham cracker crumbs and mix well. Form into 1-inch balls and chill for 1 hour.
2. In a saucepan, melt flavored frosting over low heat. Dip chilled balls in melted frosting and let dry on a rack for 6 hours.

## Louisiana Caramel Pralines

**Ingredients:**

2 cups granulated sugar
1 cup evaporated milk
1 cup granulated sugar (for melting)

2½ cups chopped pecans
(toasted, if desired)
2 Tbsp butter
1–2 tsp vanilla

**Instructions:**

1. In a large saucepan, combine 2 cups sugar and evaporated milk and cook slowly, stirring often.
2. Simultaneously, melt 1 cup of sugar in a separate saucepan over low heat, stirring constantly until it caramelizes.
3. Slowly add melted sugar to the boiling milk and sugar mixture, stirring continuously.
4. Cook until it reaches firm ball stage (238°F). Remove from heat and add butter, vanilla, and pecans.
5. Stir until mixture thickens, then drop spoonfuls onto wax paper to set.

# Beverages, Microwave, Misc.

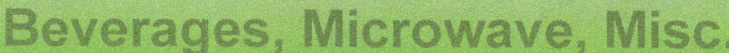

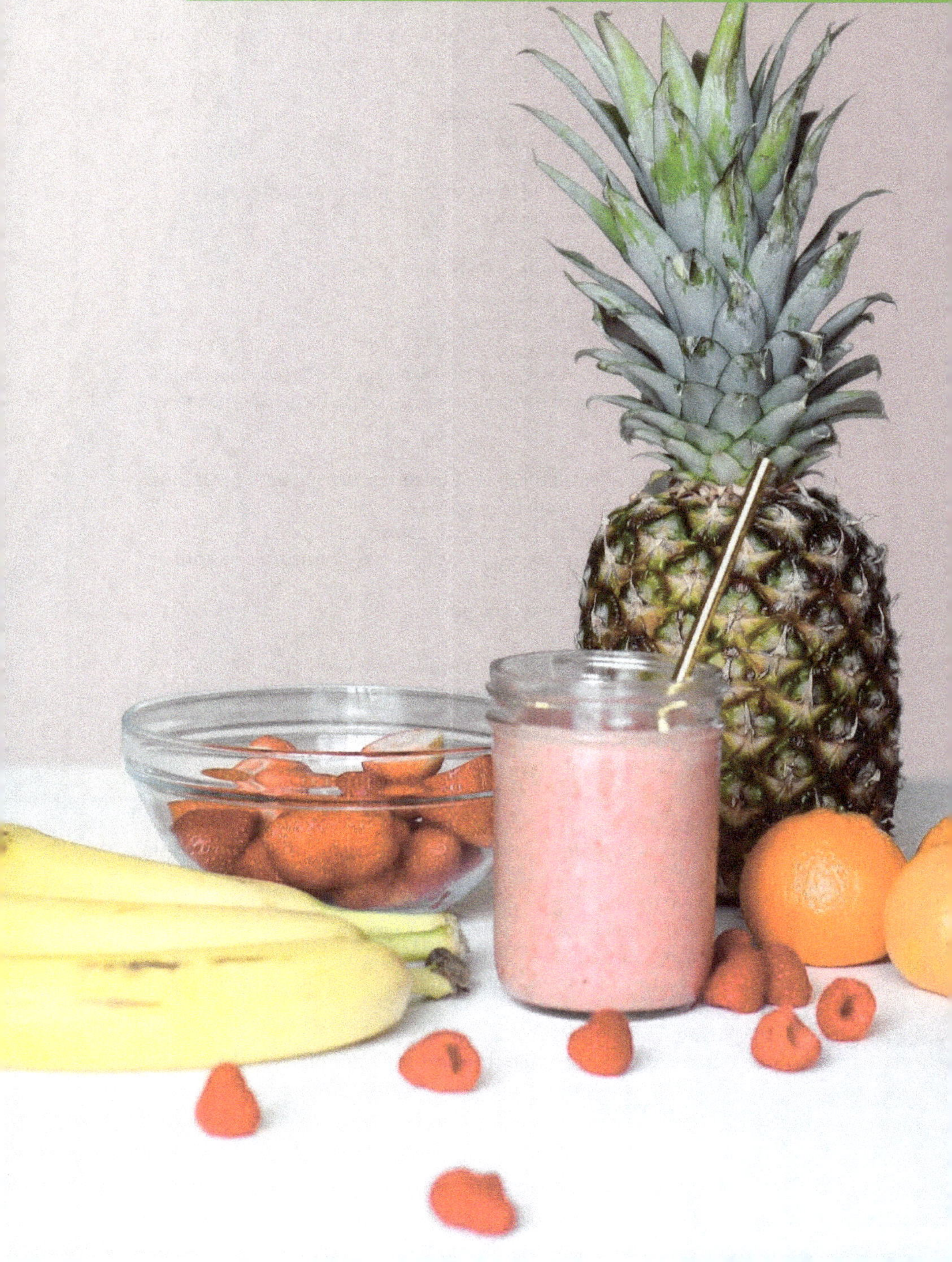

Delicious Ideas!

## Microwave Cooking Tips

1. **Softening Brown Sugar**
   - Place an open box of hardened brown sugar in the microwave with 1 cup of hot water.
   - Microwave on high:
     - **1 ½–2 minutes for ½ pound**
     - **2–3 minutes for 1 pound**
2. **Softening Butter or Margarine**
   - One stick softens in **1 minute at 20% power** in the microwave.
3. **Thawing Frozen Orange Juice**
   - Remove the metal lid.
   - Heat the opened container on high:
     - **30 seconds for 6 ounces**
     - **45 seconds for 12 ounces**
4. **Thawing Whipped Topping**
   - A 4 ½-ounce carton thaws in **1 minute on the defrost setting.**
   - The center should remain slightly firm; stir to blend. **Do not over-thaw.**
5. **Scalding Milk**
   - Cook **1 cup of milk** for **2–2 ½ minutes,** stirring once per minute.
6. **Making Dry Breadcrumbs**
   - Cut **6 slices of bread** into ½-inch cubes.
   - Microwave in a 3-quart casserole dish for **6–7 minutes** or until dry, stirring after 3 minutes.
   - Crush the dried bread in a blender.
7. **Refreshing Stale Snacks**
   - Place potato chips, crackers, or similar snacks on a plate.
   - Microwave for **30–45 seconds.** Let stand for **1 minute** to crisp.
8. **Thawing Hamburger Meat**
   - Defrost for **3 minutes,** then remove defrosted outer portions.
   - Continue defrosting in intervals, removing thawed portions as they defrost.
9. **Draining Fat from Hamburger**
   - Cook hamburger in a plastic colander placed inside a casserole dish.
   - One pound cooks in **5 minutes on high.**
10. **Microwave Baking Tips**
    - Cakes and quick breads rise higher in a microwave oven; fill pans **only halfway.**
    - Use a **round dish** instead of a square one to avoid overcooked corners.
11. **Preparing Chicken**
    - Place meaty pieces around the edges and bony pieces in the center of the dish for even cooking.
12. **Shaping Meatloaf**

- ○ Shape meatloaf into a ring to avoid an undercooked center.
- ○ Use a glass in the center of the dish as a mold.
13. **Avoid Salting Foods on the Surface**
    - ○ Salting meats and vegetables on the surface causes dehydration and toughening.
    - ○ Salt after removing the dish from the oven unless the recipe specifies adding salt during preparation.
14. **Ensuring Even Cooking**
    - ○ If the bottom of a cake or other dish isn't cooking evenly, place the dish on another plate or roasting rack.
    - ○ This tip also works for potatoes or similar foods.

# Fruit Punch Drink

*Recipe by Sharon Wolford*

**Ingredients:**

| | |
|---|---|
| 1 large can Dole pineapple juice | 1 large can frozen lemonade |
| 2 packages Kool-Aid lemon-lime | 1 quart water |
| 1 ½ cups sugar | 2 large bottles 7-Up |
| 1 large can frozen orange juice | |

**Instructions:**

1. Mix frozen juices as directed on their containers, using one less can of water for the orange juice and lemonade.
2. Combine all ingredients in a punch bowl and mix well.
3. For a festive touch, freeze punch in a Jello mold or Bundt pan to create an ice ring. Loosen ring by placing in warm water before adding to the punch.
4. Ideal for Christmas or special occasions.

# Ice Cream Drink

*Recipe by Rhea Williams*

**Ingredients:**

| | |
|---|---|
| 1-pint vanilla ice cream | ¾ cup drained, chilled sliced peaches |
| ¾ cup chilled unsweetened pineapple juice | 1 cup chilled milk |

Delicious Ideas!

**Instructions:**

1. Combine ice cream, peaches, and pineapple juice in a blender.
2. Blend until smooth.
3. Add milk and blend well.
4. Pour into chilled glasses and serve immediately.

## Tea Punch

*Recipe by Ona Goff*

**Ingredients:**

| | |
|---|---|
| 1 cup plus 2 tablespoons honey | 3 cups cold water |
| 6 cups hot strong tea | 1 ½ quarts Ginger Ale |
| 2 cups orange juice | Orange and lemon slices (for |
| 1 cup lemon juice | garnish) |

**Instructions:**

1. Dissolve honey in hot tea and let cool.
2. Add orange juice, lemon juice, and water. Strain if using fresh fruit.
3. Chill mixture thoroughly.
4. Before serving, pour into a punch bowl over ice and add Ginger Ale.
5. Garnish with orange and lemon slices.

**Yield**: 5 quarts (approximately 30 servings).

## Wedding Punch

*Recipe by Sue Cramer*

**Ingredients:**

| | |
|---|---|
| 1 (12 oz.) can frozen lemonade | 5 ripe bananas (blended well) |
| 1 (6 oz.) can frozen orange juice | 6 cups water |
| 1 large can pineapple juice | 4 cups sugar |

**Instructions:**

1. Boil sugar and water for 3 minutes; let cool.
2. Add lemonade (plus 3 cans water), orange juice, pineapple juice, and blended bananas.
3. Mix well and freeze in plastic containers.
4. When ready to serve, place frozen mixture in a punch bowl and add 7-Up.
5. You can tint the punch to match wedding colors before freezing.

**Serves**: Approximately 50.

# Cider Punch

*Recipe by Ona Goff*

**Ingredients:**

2 quarts cider (or apple juice)
1 quart Ginger Ale
6 (3-inch) cinnamon sticks
12 cloves
1 (1 lb. 13 oz.) can crushed
pineapple

1 (1 lb. 4 oz.) can pineapple juice
6 cups orange juice
2 cups lemon juice
Orange slices (for garnish)
Maraschino cherry halves
(optional garnish)

**Instructions:**

1. Simmer cider with cinnamon sticks and cloves for about 15 minutes; let cool and remove spices.
2. Chill all juices thoroughly.
3. Combine all ingredients in a punch bowl with a block of ice or an ice ring.
4. Garnish with orange slices and cherries, if desired.

**Yield**: About 5 quarts (approximately 30 servings).

# All Occasion Punch

*Recipe by Eva Jordan*

**Ingredients:**

2 (46 oz.) cans red Hawaiian
Punch
1 (46 oz.) can pineapple juice
½ cup lemon juice

2 quarts lemon-lime soda
(chilled)
Lemon and orange slices (for
garnish)

**Instructions:**

1. Combine all ingredients in a punch bowl just before serving.
2. Pour over ice and garnish with lemon and orange slices.
3. For extra punch, freeze additional mixture in ice trays or rings.

**Serves**: Approximately 50.

Delicious Ideas!

## Kool-Aid 7-Up Cooler*

*Recipe by Ona Goff*

**Ingredients:**

1 small packet lemon-flavored Kool-Aid
1 small packet strawberry-flavored Kool-Aid

1 small packet fruit punch-flavored Kool-Aid
1 (46 oz.) can pineapple juice, chilled
3 cans 7-Up, chilled

**Instructions:**

1. Prepare Kool-Aid according to package directions.
2. Just before serving, add chilled 7-Up and pineapple juice.
3. Stir gently and serve.

***Alternative:** Substitute Fanta (red pop) or Red Cream Soda for 7-Up for a different flavor.

## Popsicles

*Recipe by Ona Goff*

**Ingredients:**

1 (3 oz.) package orange-flavored gelatin
2 cups boiling water

2 cups orange juice
½ cup sugar

**Instructions:**

1. Dissolve gelatin and sugar in boiling water.
2. Stir in orange juice.
3. Pour mixture into ice cube trays, paper cups, or popsicle molds.
4. Freeze for 2–3 hours. For popsicle sticks, insert them after 45–60 minutes.

***Note:** Strawberry gelatin with cranberry juice or lemon gelatin with lemonade are delicious variations.

## Deviled Pork Marinade

*Recipe by Ona Goff*

**Ingredients:**

3 tablespoons chili sauce
1 ½ tablespoons lemon juice
1 tablespoon grated onion
2 teaspoons Worcestershire sauce

½ teaspoon salt
¼ teaspoon dry mustard
¼ teaspoon paprika
⅛ teaspoon curry powder

**Instructions:**

1. Mix all ingredients well.
2. Marinate pork for several hours or overnight, turning frequently.
3. Ideal for pork steaks, fresh sliced shoulder, or pork chops.

## Steak Marinade

*Recipe by Ona Goff*

**Ingredients:**

¼ cup salad oil
¼ cup brown sugar
2 tablespoons dry mustard
2 tablespoons Worcestershire
sauce

2 tablespoons prepared
horseradish
2 teaspoons hot pepper sauce
Unseasoned meat tenderizer

**Instructions:**

1. Combine all ingredients except tenderizer.
2. Sprinkle tenderizer on meat before cooking.
3. Marinate meat for at least 8 hours or overnight, turning every 2–3 hours.

## Shrimp Cocktail Sauce

*Recipe by Ona Goff*

**Ingredients:**

1 cup chili sauce
3 tablespoons prepared
horseradish

1 tablespoon lemon juice
Hot pepper sauce to taste
Salt and pepper to taste

**Instructions:**

1. Mix all ingredients well.
2. Refrigerate until ready to serve.

## Barbecue Sauce

*Recipe by Doris Mooney*

### Ingredients:

¼ cup vinegar
1 teaspoon dry mustard
2 tablespoons brown sugar
1 tablespoon liquid smoke
1 can tomato juice
½ cup water
¼ cup ketchup

2 tablespoons Worcestershire sauce
1 teaspoon chili powder
1 tablespoon paprika
Dash of hot sauce
1 teaspoon salt
¼ teaspoon pepper

### Instructions:

1. Combine dry ingredients, then add wet ingredients.
2. Bring to a boil and serve.

## Barbecue Sauce

*Recipe by Beverly Rose*

### Ingredients:

1 cup ketchup
2 tablespoons Worcestershire sauce
2 tablespoons vinegar

2 tablespoons sugar
½ teaspoon salt
½ teaspoon liquid smoke
Few grains red or black pepper

### Instructions:

1. Mix all ingredients in order listed.
2. Makes 1 pint.

## Tartar Sauce

*Recipe by Ona Goff*

### Ingredients:

1 cup mayonnaise
2 tablespoons chopped dill pickle
or sweet pickle relish, drained
2 tablespoons lemon juice
1 tablespoon chopped parsley

1 tablespoon capers
1 teaspoon grated onion
1 tablespoon finely chopped celery

**Instructions:**

1. Combine all ingredients in a small bowl.
2. Chill before serving.

## Popcorn Balls

*Recipe by Winifred Bondurant*

**Ingredients:**

2 cups sugar
⅔ cup light corn syrup
⅔ cup water
½ cup margarine

2 teaspoons salt
1 ½ teaspoons vanilla
5–6 quarts popped corn

**Instructions:**

1. Mix sugar, corn syrup, water, margarine, and salt in a saucepan.
2. Cook until mixture is brittle when dropped in cold water (270°F).
3. Stir in vanilla.
4. Pour mixture over popped corn. Grease hands with margarine and form into balls.
5. Yields 18–24 popcorn balls.

## Caramel Corn

*Recipe by Shirley Chaffin*

**Ingredients:**

2 cups brown sugar, packed
½ cup dark corn syrup
1 cup margarine

½ teaspoon cream of tartar
1 teaspoon soda
6 quarts popped corn

**Instructions:**

1. Combine brown sugar, syrup, margarine, and cream of tartar in a saucepan.
2. Bring to a hard boil, stirring constantly. Boil for 5 minutes.
3. Remove from heat and stir in soda.
4. Pour over popcorn and mix well.
5. Bake at 250°F for 1 hour, stirring occasionally.
6. Store in airtight containers.

## Caramel Popcorn

*Recipe by Rhea Williams*

**Ingredients**:

15 cups popped corn
½ cup brown sugar
½ cup butter or margarine
¼ cup light corn syrup

½ teaspoon salt
½ teaspoon soda
½ teaspoon vanilla

**Instructions**:

1. Preheat oven to 200°F.
2. Spread popped corn in two 9x12-inch baking pans.
3. In a saucepan, combine sugar, butter, syrup, vanilla, and salt. Cook over medium heat until mixture starts to boil.
4. Boil for 5 minutes, then stir in soda until foamy.
5. Pour mixture evenly over popcorn and stir.
6. Bake for 1 hour, stirring every 15 minutes.

# index

**Formerly Referred to as The Morning Star Missionaries**
is the Women's ministry at Agape International Cathedral; (Prior church name was Morning Star Tabernacle).

The mission of S.E.E.D. (Sisters Empowered and Equipped for Destiny) is to nurture wholeness in women by taking a holistic approach through edification in the offering of programs designed to minister spiritual, physical, cognitive, emotional and social needs. Through worship, fellowship and discipleship, we foster in the love of Christ in our commitment to serve and support one another.

Agape International Cathedral

**Bishop Dr. Marcus A McIntosh, Pastor**

**Agape S.E.E.D. Ministry Staff**
**Evangelist Sheila Collins**
*President*
**Sister Diana Biyani**
*Vice-President*
**Sister Tonya Price**
*Secretary*

S.E.E.D.

You may order as many copies of our cookbook as you wish. Cost is $20 per book. If you would like your book(s) to be mailed, please include $3.50 for S&H or just stop by the church for pickup. Mail order to:

Agape International Cathedral
c/o Sheila Collins. S.E.E.D. Ministry
85 Eaton Street
Delaware, OH 43015

Qty _____   Pickup ☐   Delivery ☐

Name _____

Addr. _____

City _____ State _____ Zip _____

Email _____

Ph: _____

To Place Your Order, Visit Our Website at
www.agapeic.org

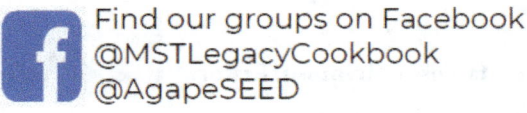
Find our groups on Facebook
@MSTLegacyCookbook
@AgapeSEED